HIDDEN SHAME

HIDDEN SHAME

The Shocking Story of America's Elderly Ill

Margarite Alvarez
and Judy Higgerson, R.N.,
with David McIntyre

WITHDRAWN

VANTAGE PRESS
New York • Los Angeles

FIRST EDITION

Copyright © 1990 by Margarite Alvarez and Judy Higgerson, R.N.

Published by Vantage Press, Inc.
516 West 34th Street, New York, New York 10001

Manufactured in the United States of America
ISBN: 0-533-09023-7

Library of Congress Catalog Card No.:
90-90063

1 2 3 4 5 6 7 8 9 0

To my mother, Margarita Wuthrich, with love and gratitude.

—Margarite Alvarez

To my grandparents, Bess and Bill Wolfe, who instilled in me the self-confidence to accomplish all my goals.

—Judy Higgerson

At eighty-one years of age he had enough lucidity to realize that he was attached to this world by a few slender threads that could break painlessly with a simple change of position while he slept, and if he did all he could do to keep those threads intact, it was because of his terror of not finding God in the darkness of death.

Gabriel Garcia Marquez
Love in the Time of Cholera

"It ain't dyin' I'm talking about, it's living," Augustus said. *"I doubt it matters where you die, but it matters where you live."*

Larry McMurtry
Lonesome Dove

Contents

Foreword

I am glad Ms. Alvarez and Ms. Higgerson have come out with this book, as disturbing as parts of it may be. These two professionals, involved in the business of health care, have recorded stories of the human side of health care. And, while they have focused on seniors who live in California, the plight of these people can be seen all over the country. The authors of *Hidden Shame* confront us with a picture of American health care for the elderly, warts and all. The book reminds us of how far America still must go in order to ensure access to high-quality, affordable health care.

The gaps in our health care system are deeply disturbing. We are arguably the richest nation in the world, with an abundance of resources, and yet over 1 million of our citizens annually become bankrupt trying to meet the costs of long-term care. With the exception of Medicaid, the Federal-State health program for the very needy, neither private nor public insurance provides any meaningful protection from the costs of such chronic health problems as Alzheimer's disease, cancer, Parkinson's disease and stroke.

I applaud these authors for urging our country to chart a course away from institutionalization, and toward ensuring the health care so critical to the quality of life of our citizens. I think anyone with an elderly friend or relative, or anyone who's elderly or on the way to that honored status, will find this interesting reading.

—Congressman Claude Pepper

Throughout my career in Congress, I have taken an active interest in the health and well-being of the elderly and their need for compassionate, cost-effective community-based care. This interest has led me to propose a number of measures on home care, adult day care, and hospice care, some of which have been enacted.

Now, three residents of California's 16th Congressional District, which I represent and which covers much of central California's coastal region, have written a book on the elderly and the need for home care. Its core consists of a number of case histories of the elderly, their families, and others who need home or long-term care. Most of these case histories describe people and situations from Carmel and the Monterey Peninsula, which are in my district, and relate the difficulties that many elderly and their caretakers face when illness strikes, health deteriorates, or finances worsen.

The book's title, *Hidden Shame*, effectively describes one main point of these case histories: that many elderly in the Monterey area, and elsewhere in the country, live lives of misery, poverty, and neglect associated with chronic illness or declining health. The other important point is that much of this misery could be lessened or even totally avoided through better information and greater access to affordable, quality in-home care.

Institutional care, while expensive, is clearly appropriate and necessary for some of our older citizens. However, it makes no sense to emphasize or encourage institutional care for all elderly Americans. It has been clearly demonstrated that we have resources available to provide cost-effective, compassionate alternatives through a range of services that enable the elderly to remain in their homes and communities even if they are quite ill and disabled. As the number of elderly in the United States continues to grow, meeting their long-term health care needs will be a challenge for our present system. Just as the aged must not be left without adequate health care, they also should not be forced into one living situation.

Home care, and other community-based care such as adult day care, enables the elderly to remain in homes and communities where many of them have lived much or even all of their lives. It allows them to stay close to family, as well as to friends and neighbors they have known for many years. It is obvious that not being forced to be uprooted from one's natural surroundings is good for one's outlook and mental well-being; there is much evidence that this is also good for one's physical condition as well.

While in Congress, I have sponsored legislation to improve and expand home care services under Medicare, establish a Medicare adult day care benefit, and establish and then make permanent a Medicare hospice benefit. These types of community-based care are important not only for their compassionate aspects, but for their cost-effectiveness as well. In a time when rapidly rising health care costs are posing an increasing burden for citizens as well as governments, it is essential that new programs save costs while providing better health care.

Our country faces a major challenge in seeking to care for our nation's elderly, and to do so in ways that preserve their dignity and, where possible, enable them to remain in their own homes and communities. We must move forward with necessary reforms to ensure that quality health care will be available and affordable for the growing elderly population, as well as for all other American citizens. As the nation considers long-term care and overall health care proposals, the utilization of cost-effective and humane alternatives like home care should be a significant component of our policy and program. We must take action to try to ensure that old age is something which is looked forward to, rather than dreaded, by our growing elderly population.

—Congressman Leon E. Panetta

Preface

A little over six years ago, my partner, Judy Higgerson, a registered nurse, and I opened our business doors for the first time, I had no knowledge of the home health-care field and no medical or nursing background. I was the so-called business partner, handling the financial, legal, data processing, promotional, and marketing aspects.

At times, because there were only two of us at the start, I had to help Judy do consultations, contact physicians, and develop staffing resources. It was during these times that I soon came to realize how poorly our health-care system provides for us and, most especially, for our elderly.

Being in my mid-thirties, these were concerns that had not been realized in my life, except for the death of my father after a very short illness. And, except for that brief period, he had never suffered a chronic or debilitating illness that created a loss of independence for him or hardship on my brother or me. He had about $10,000 when he died and we used that to pay his medical bills. I shudder to think of the thousands upon thousands of dollars of medical expense that my brother and I would have accumulated had my father not died so quickly.

It was only six months into our business that I said to Judy that we had material for a book—the clients we cared for, the families we talked to, all frustrated and confused, all bereft and devastated by the emotional impact and the financial drain.

Almost all had one thing in common: They had not planned for themselves or their loved ones, they did not know how to handle the situations in which they found themselves, and they were all shocked to find the cost was to be mostly borne by them.

I had grown up in a beautiful community, I had a good business and good skills and education. My family, though far from wealthy, was comfortable. I had insurance. I would *never* have realized how little any of this meant had I not gotten into this field. I probably would not have known until another family member became ill or until I myself became older and in need of assistance. And then I would have found myself having the same problems, with the same frustrations and fears, as all these people I was now seeing.

It was truly a terrifying thought that even well-educated and reasonably affluent people could very easily find themselves in situations about which they had no forethought, knowledge, or finances to cope.

Understanding the problems of demographics and population-age shifts that we will be experiencing in the coming years, I realize that aging will affect *all of us* at some time, in a traumatic way.

Even more frightening was the realization that, because of the direction our health-care system is taking, because of the lack of expectation, because of the lack of forethought, because of the denial of the reality of aging, because of ignorance, chances are any one of us—including baby boomers and those who follow us—will face not six months to two years in a nursing home, but an average of four to eight years of our lives in a nursing-home environment.

For any of you who have not been in such a home (and I am not speaking of a retirement community, but a nursing home or convalescent hospital), I suggest you spend a day or two in one and see if this is how you hope to spend up to a decade of your life.

No matter how much care you take of your diet and exercise, nothing can stop the total effects of aging. We are trying to live as long as possible with better health care of our bodies, but that does not mean we will not at some time suffer breakdowns, and we will begin to have some problems that will create a need for some assistance.

If the quality of your life is important, read this book; learn, plan, and begin to act. The warning is here. The book has now been written. It is up to us, all of us, to start planning for our complete future.

Margarite Alvarez
2-24-90

Acknowledgments

We wish to acknowledge the following people: Margarita and Fred Wuthrich, Goldie and Ret. Colonel George Van Way, and Pat and Ted Bazett for their support and, most especially, for their trust; Lynne Sullivan, the Roberts Family, Martha Douglas, Kerry Arnett, Cissie Brewer, as professionals and friends, who encouraged us always; our staff, which provided us with loyalty, time, and dedication; and all nurses and caregivers throughout the country, because they do the real work.

HIDDEN SHAME

1. America's Hidden Shame

ANDRE AND MARIE

You wouldn't be likely to look twice if you had seen Andre and Marie walking along Ocean Avenue, the main street of famed Carmel-by-the-Sea, California.

Although they would not be mistaken for tourists as they strolled, apparently window-shopping, there was nothing in their rather plain, elderly appearance that drew attention. Yet they were among the community's most prosperous citizens. In fact, over the years they had purchased and now owned a great deal of real estate in and around Carmel.

Andre and Marie were classmates as young people, then lovers, and eventually husband and wife. After some time, they were divorced, childless. But their joint business interests kept them together. As the years passed, they became more and more reclusive. Now in their eighties, they resided in separate small apartments above commercial properties they owned.

Their only interests were each other and their business ventures. When Marie began to develop Alzheimer's disease, not knowing what was happening, Andre tried to ignore it. To outsiders, they conducted their lives as usual and no one who knew them knew of anything unusual.

One day, during a walk, Marie fell. Andre helped her up to her apartment. A shopkeeper, aware of Marie's age and concerned about her fall, called us to look into the situation. He suspected Marie had been hurt.

We went to Marie's apartment, knocked on the door and, when there was no answer, summoned the police. They forced entry and discovered Marie sitting in a pool of blood on the sofa, hemorrhaging, probably as a result of her fall. Marie's fingernails were several inches long and beginning to curl under. Discarded aluminum TV-dinner trays were stacked to the ceiling, everywhere. Mice ran freely across the floor. The sight to most people would have been something one might expect to see in a horror movie, not in the middle of Carmel.

We immediately got her to the hospital and Andre accompanied her. Within a few days, a distant family member came to town and signed papers to have Marie sent to a convalescent hospital.

No other options were discussed and she was admitted. By the second day, Andre had barricaded the doors, would let no one into her room. He insisted that she would have to go home and that there was no way he was going to allow her to stay there.

The family member finally acquiesced. Andre and Marie had no attorneys and no bank trust officer to look after their interests. The had always handled their affairs themselves.

Marie was in an advanced stage of Alzheimer's at this point. Andre simply didn't understand what had happened to her or the nature of the disease. He tried to shelter her and take care of her himself. Andre was terrified of the circumstance and of the prospect that they might somehow be split up. They had only each other. He looked to us for help.

We explained that we could not just come in and take over, that he would have to deal with an attorney and things would have to be set up for her in order to make decisions. He agreed to appoint a conservator, but the distant relative resisted and fought the effort.

The conservator, without foreknowledge of the situation, was somewhat at a loss as to how to deal with it. He wanted to cut costs by hiring other agencies at less expense.

Eventually, we managed to establish some balance. But the relative then reentered the picture and began to make changes in things like the kind and dosage of vitamins Marie was taking. He finally called the doctor and got him to make some medicinal changes for Marie without the doctor ever seeing her. The conservator, not wanting to disagree with the relative, allowed this to happen.

When we found out what was going on, we called the doctor. He refused to return our phone calls. Then we made an appointment to see the doctor in his office. When we approached the doctor to discuss the relative's motives, including the relative's order to the nurse on duty to literally stop feeding Marie, the doctor threw us out of the office without responding to our concerns. We subsequently discovered that Marie's relative and her doctor were involved together in several business ventures.

We then confronted the conservator with the information we had. He changed doctors and adhered to Andre's wishes as Marie's long-time companion, former husband, and business partner, retaining us to care for Marie. After several years, the relative ef-

3

fectively managed to change the caregiver relationship for Marie. She died within six months.

FLORENCE

Florence is ninety-two years old, just about five feet tall, and what one might call a soft-spoken "Southern charmer." A teacher in her youth, she still dresses crisply in a colorful sweater and skirt. Alert and decidedly not old fashioned, she credits her general frame of mind to the fact that she has kept alert to what's happening in the world and, for many years, has enjoyed the company of "young people," as she refers to almost anyone.

Florence lives with her daughter and son-in-law, both in their sixties. Their home, a comfortable two-story house in a lovely setting, is in Carmel Valley, near Carmel-by-the-Sea.

On the surface, the situation seems ideal. To the neighbors, Florence's dutiful daughter is taking care of her mother, just as a dutiful daughter should be. The fact that the neighbors haven't seen Florence in a number of months doesn't seem unusual. Florence, after all, is elderly. She probably wishes to remain inside.

Behind the closed door, the story is different. Florence is a virtual prisoner in her daughter's home. She is confined to a single room on the second floor and is told by her daughter in no uncertain terms that she is not to leave her room unattended.

Her daughter is concerned that as a result of an accident several years ago, when Florence fell and broke her hip, and because her eyesight has been failing, she may fall again while the daughter is out of the house.

Florence's daughter keeps her confined to the second floor because the daughter's husband has cancer and is convalescing in a bedroom on the first floor. The daughter has chosen not to tell Florence about the cancer, not wanting to alarm her.

The fact that her daughter is often gone for hours at a time, that the daughter's attitude seems to have changed in recent months, and that she appears to be living under a threat, frightens Florence. Her gentile Southern upbringing and her natural inclination to avoid confrontation prevent Florence from discussing the subject. At the same time, she doesn't understand her daughter's apparent lack of concern for her.

Florence's story is not unusual. In countless cases across our nation, people with parents or other loved ones for whom they cannot or will not provide proper care, or because of a lack of information on options available to them, are creating circumstances that constitute a form of hidden shame. They are putting older loved ones in desperate circumstances that often create ill will, feelings of guilt, shame, and emotional separation.

The cause? A combination of more people living longer, the escalating cost of health care, the increasing number of two-worker families, and the carrying of old baggage filled with "shoulds and oughts" regarding how elderly loved ones are to be cared for.

The result? We are creating family care problems with which people are not equipped to deal. We thereby condemn increasing numbers of elderly and infirm loved ones to lives needlessly complicated by human actions, which—though often well intended—are nevertheless inadequate and often ill advised. These actions frequently are controlled by guilt, anxiety, ignorance, and shame.

THE REALITIES OF AGING

The Committee on Aging of the House of Representatives has reported that there were 27.5 million Americans over sixty-five in the United States in 1980. That figure is projected to increase to 40 million by the year 2000 and 64 million by 2030—one person in five. By that time, fully 22 percent of our population will be over age sixty-five.

At the same time, as people live longer, they also have a tendency to develop increasing health-care needs. Fifty years ago we didn't have the means to treat cancer and heart disease that we do now. Polio and tuberculosis, major causes of death prior to World War II, are virtually nonexistent in the U.S. today. The average life span in 1930 was sixty-three years. People didn't recover from many serious illnesses; they simply died. Today, medical advances have increased our average life span to seventy-five and it continues to expand!

The change, though welcome, has not come without new problems. As people live longer, they are increasingly likely to require medical care for more maladies than fifty years ago. As medical technology has advanced, so has the cost of providing medical care. We will live longer, but the cost will be higher. Not all of us will be able to afford it.

ge layoffs are occurring in the manufacturing
farmers are losing their farms in record num-
banks are closing, and service industries are
low wages, with meager benefits. In many
communities, unemployment is more than 35
t. Many people are not protected by any form
alth insurance, let alone comprehensive
ge. Even comprehensive coverage will not
most in-home assistance needs.

r people approaching what have been called the
years," the joyous prospect of living longer is
empered by the fearsome prospect of doing so
ected from the ravages of income-draining
-care expenses. The prospect is not appealing.

CARE

me health care was something taken for granted
generations ago when families lived together,
ntly had numerous children, and women were
ed to be homemakers and caregivers. It is now
test-growing segment of the rapidly expanding
-care industry. The difference between then
ow is that most home care today is provided by
outside the family and it is costly.

ke any new and expanding industry, the home
-care field is having growing pains. It is in a
where often unforeseen problems have made
uneven and not without the need for adjust-
For instance, many needs of older people that
attention are being provided for by untrained
makers." Too frequently, such people are
t of as a relatively inexpensive panacea and

EMMA

Emma is seventy-two and seriously overweight.
She is forgetful. She lives alone in a simple apartment and spends most of her time reading or watch-
ing television. Her son, an enlisted man in the navy,
is stationed halfway around the world.

Several months ago she entered the hospital for
treatment of a diabetic condition. When her condition
was stabilized, she was sent home. With no one to
look after her, and without help, the concern was
that her condition would revert within a matter of
weeks to what it was when she was admitted. She is
a proud woman who, recognizing her forgetfulness
and the fact that she lives alone, is developing increasing anxiety.

Emma's son is not only apparently unaware of
her condition, there is little he could do if he were. His
military health-care program does not cover Emma.

Emma is one of the growing number of cases
where nothing can be done. She is not indigent, but
cannot afford the cost of a nurse's assistant. Her son
is not able to help her financially. She does not
qualify for Medicare assistance because the care she
needs does not require a skilled nurse. She cannot
drive a car, so she has trouble doing shopping and
running errands. Her case is not uncommon.

Medicare coverage provides for (A) hospitalization
and (B) supplementary medical care. As recently as
1984, part B of the Medicare program paid $1.8 bil-
lion for home health care.

Why then is Emma (and thousands like her) not
covered? Because Medicare covers physician's visits
and, to some degree, services of a registered nurse,

not those of nurses' assistants or licensed vocational nurses (LVNs) except when in conjunction with skilled nursing care and then only for brief periods.

It covers some costs of ambulance service, diagnostic testing, physical and speech therapy, prosthetic devices, and other medical equipment.

In large measure, Medicare works for people like Emma while they are hospitalized. However, changes in regulations that relate to reimbursement of hospital expenses have forced hospitals to release many patients earlier than five years ago. Thus, they leave "quicker and sicker," usually requiring convalescent or in-home care where, in the past, they used to be discharged "when well enough to go home and function close to normally."

So while technology allows us to live longer, the cost of maintaining that healthy lifestyle has increased to the point where, even with comprehensive health-insurance coverage, many people are finding it difficult to maintain their health because of the costs involved. Unfortunately, Emma ended up back in the hospital not long after her discharge. She needn't have. The doctor, the hospital, and her son are all frustrated and another human life may well be shortened because there is a hole in the safety net. Emma has cause to be frightened.

THE REALITY OF MEDICARE

"Oh well, we're covered by Medicare" is the all-too-frequent and complacent rejoinder of many older people as they face the prospect of hospitalization and recuperation.

"The reality," according to dinator at Community Hospita Peninsula, in California, "is tha shocked to find that Medicare d deal of the care they will requir hospital. It is sad to have to con reality of what is not covered."

And what do these people fir hospital? They often find that exc ing care over short periods, very li is true even when the physicia acute care. For many people ther And for many the cost, both finan ly, to themselves or relatives, can

In many communities there a convalescent care homes. People r must be moved to communities re commutes for relatives and friends visits.

Fortunately, in more and n across the nation, in-home care created that provide an excellent a ing or convalescent homes.

Unfortunately, however, many as in any new field, are *not* licen monitored to assure they are prov care to patient/clients.

THE GOLDEN YEARS

While the federal government t people are employed than ever bef barded by stories in the news mec

that i
secto
bers,
payin
urba
perce
of h
cover
cover

"gold
often
unpr
heal

HOM

seve
freq
exp
the
hea
and
peo

hea
sta
gro
me
re
"h
th

the real needs of the patient are not covered.

BILL

For example, Bill was a well-educated, reasonably affluent professional man of seventy-two. Jaunty, slightly on the stout side, he was given to wearing golf sweaters and a little hat. Bill has been regarded as affable, with a good sense of humor.

Bill had a heart attack and was hospitalized. When he was ready for discharge, the doctor who treated him specified Bill needed someone "to sit with him." The physician did not ask for someone with nursing training. As a result, Bill got a companion, someone who would not have known what to do if Bill had another attack, developed some other medical problem, or failed to take his medicine as prescribed. Bill's son, also a physician, is not a cardiovascular specialist. Neither the physician son nor Bill's discharging doctor knew enough about home-care options available to Bill to prescribe someone knowledgeable about Bill's medical condition and able to respond appropriately if the need arose.

After several weeks, Bill suffered multiple seizures. The companion, not knowing what to do, did nothing. Fortunately, Bill's son stopped by to see his father at this point and, discovering what had happened, called the 911 emergency number and had his father taken to the hospital.

Questioning the companion, Bill's son learned she had not been trained how to react in an emergency and, in actuality, had not even recognized the symptoms of the seizures.

While recovering in the hospital, the son, with

11

the assistance of the hospital, obtained another companion; again someone with no medical background.

When Bill had another seizure and pulled out the tubes and I.V.s that were required at the time, the companion simply sat by and watched. Again, Bill's son happened to stop in to see his father and discovered what had happened. He demanded to know why the "sitter" had not notified the floor nurse. The individual replied it wasn't her job. "I'm just paid to sit here," she replied.

She was quickly replaced by someone with medical training from our agency and both the physician and the hospital learned a valuable lesson.

A home health aide from our agency was obtained to care for Bill at home when he was discharged.

The physician son by this time had become aware of the difference in skills and training from caregivers in various agencies in the area.

Bill is now at home. Once easygoing and flexible, he has become stubborn and sullen as a result of his condition and the neglect suffered through unreliable care. He refuses to use a walker and has fallen a number of times. He also refuses to exercise and thus his muscles are atrophying. The blood flow to his extremities is poor.

If Bill had caregivers who reacted properly when his seizures occurred, chances are good he would not have suffered debilitating setbacks.

The problem? Neither the son, a physician, or the daughter, a homemaker, took the time or made the effort to find out what options were available to their dad before the need became critical. Thus he, and they, have gone through a number of unpleasant experiences which might have been avoided.

Sound unusual? It isn't.

ELIZABETH

Elizabeth is a large woman of apparent Slavic background, with thick hands and a weathered face. She wears heavy, laced shoes. On our initial visit to her, one shoe had an opening cut in it to relieve a bunion. Quietly stoic, her eyes showed a character both strong and determined.

Elizabeth had a pulmonary problem and high blood pressure. A widow, she was tenaciously clinging to a house too large for her to care for. She continued to do her laundry in the sink on a scrub board. Her only living relative was a bookish, seemingly indecisive nephew.

As a result of a series of illnesses, Elizabeth had been seeing several doctors and had received prescriptions from each. None of her physicians was aware of the prescriptions of the others. In addition, Elizabeth had recently lost her husband and was in a state of acute depression.

The attorney handling her husband's estate assured Elizabeth he would attend to everything. He showed no interest in her medical problems, assuming that her doctors were on top of that aspect. He often left her confused with explanations of things with which he was involved.

Finally, when Elizabeth was seriously confused and the results of her mixed medicines and depression were beginning to take their toll, a neighbor, concerned about Elizabeth and alerted to a decline in her physical condition by a friend who is a nurse, called us.

We were warned that Elizabeth might not be receptive to our visit because of her state of mind, caused by drugs and depression over the loss of her spouse.

When we arrived at her home, we immediately discovered that there were problems with her medications. She had bottles dating back to 1946 still sitting in her medicine cabinet.

The nephew, who had been living with Elizabeth only a few weeks and who had had no contact with her for many years, seemed unable or unwilling to take charge of his aunt's life. Only the neighbors had been able to recognize something was seriously wrong and take action.

We contacted Elizabeth's doctor, who had been treating her concerns over the phone rather than in person. He discovered she had been seeing other doctors and, after conferring with his colleagues, straightened out her medications. Elizabeth subsequently was sent to the hospital.

But for Elizabeth it was too late. Neglect and lack of understanding of the options had placed her in an irreversible situation. She was sent to a nursing home from the hospital and ultimately died there. The home of which she was so proud became part of her estate and eventually was sold at auction.

Someone who might have been able to help Elizabeth was her late husband's lawyer. Although he apparently was doing a good job in handling her finances and legal affairs, he did not see that her physical condition needed attention, nor did he press

14

the nephew to action when the nephew arrived on the scene.

Home health care, provided by a qualified agency, could have helped Florence, Emma, Bill, and Elizabeth. It is helping millions of Americans who have conditions caused by mental or physical impairment that can be treated in the home.

WHAT IS HOME HEALTH CARE?

The American Medical Association defines *home health care* as "any arrangement for providing, under medical supervision, needed health care or supportive services to a sick or disabled person in his/her own home surroundings."

Why home care?

Home care is an important option because the patient is usually happier and more comfortable in his/her own home and learns to live more independently at home than in a hospital. Being at home allows him/her to live in familiar surroundings, often near friends and relatives.

Allowing a patient to live at home with appropriate help also permits loved ones responsible for the patient to conduct their lives in a more normal, more guilt-free manner.

Today we can take care of almost anyone at home. From simple personal hygiene to highly technical skilled care, we have the capability to keep people out of nursing homes.

TOM

Says Tom, a soft-spoken, deeply tanned rancher from Salinas, California, an agricultural town east of Carmel, "I could see it coming. I knew my mother was going to be a problem. She is an independent cuss just like the rest of us. She made us promise we wouldn't put her in a nursing home and we said we wouldn't. But putting up with her in our home was another matter. If we did that, pretty soon she'd be running our home the way she ran her own. And that would be pretty tough on my wife and kids . . . and on our marriage.

"But with her problems, she couldn't live alone out there in the valley.

"So we worked out the alternatives. She could go to a residential care home and live with some other folks her age who needed care. She wouldn't hear of it. She could move in with my brother. She didn't like that idea, thank goodness.

"When we suggested she have someone stay with her during the day, getting her meals, monitoring her medicines, and seeing that she got to the doctor's and out on a tour of the ranch each day, she wasn't too keen on that either. But the idea of being able to stay in her own home was appealing.

"Well, when the first companion was hired, Mom was no pleasure to be around. Always a fiesty number, she really protested. She'd throw things and really make a fuss. At the same time, she needed someone to look after her. She wouldn't comb her hair or take a bath or things like that. I didn't know what we were going to do. It was tough. After a few days, the first companion was gone.

16

"Through a friend, we heard of Country Home Care. When we talked to them, they told us the first person often didn't work out because the idea was new to the individual requiring care. A stranger in the house often wasn't well received. But the seed would be planted and the next person might be more welcome.

"They pointed out the value of an outside, objective party and this helped take some of the emotion out of the situation.

"Carol, the next woman who showed up, was born and raised on a ranch, just like Mom. Pretty soon they hit it off. Mom was more receptive and now, after six weeks, she's become just like a member of the family. I guess Mom also thought about the fact that if she didn't give in a little, she'd have to go to a convalescent hospital.

"Mom's health has improved to the point where she only needs four or five hours of help a day, four days a week. We can pick up the rest. And she feels more independent, looks forward to Carol's visits and everyone is happy."

Not all home health-care stories have this kind of happy ending. An important point here is the need for a blending of the personality of the caregiver with that of the patient/client.

Many communities do not yet have home health-care services and, in some cases, those that exist are marginal in the quality of evaluation and care they provide. There are and will remain abuses in this fast-growing industry.

When we need to be in a hospital, we are aware of that need. The problem becomes acute and there is little question as to where to turn. When we are discharged from the hospital, our physician, or the discharge planner at most hospitals, will spell out our options, usually a convalescent or nursing care home, a residential-care facility, or home health care by an individual or agency providing that service.

Usually the patient or the patient's relative or friend is confronted with the need to select an appropriate facility or agency. Most of us are woefully ill-equipped to do so and usually we have to make such decisions with short or no lead time.

"Your father will be discharged tomorrow," you are told. "He will have to go to a convalescent home. There are three in the area. Which would you prefer?" Sometimes you have little choice. The number of homes with available beds limits the options. Sometimes costs limit the options; sometimes location or appearance.

Similarly, you hear, "Your father will be discharged tomorrow. We have seven or ten or a dozen home health-care services. We cannot make recommendations. Which would you prefer? We will be happy to contact the one you choose in your behalf."

It is difficult enough to choose an agency in a community in which you are already a resident. It becomes infinitely more difficult to make the choice if the community is unfamiliar; if you live in one part of the country and your loved one lives in another, for instance.

But this situation is confronting more and more people as adults live longer, require care for some form of mental or physical infirmity, and as we continue to live apart from our older loved ones.

DAVID

"I am the oldest of four children," notes David, a well-groomed, gray-haired, professional man living on the West Coast. "Each of my siblings has a family. I am divorced and my family is grown. Therefore—and because it is my nature—it has fallen upon me to take the lead in looking into options for my father who lives in Florida and is in his eighties.

"Over the past several years, I have made trips to visit my father and have been quietly looking into some of the options in his home community regarding residential-care homes, nursing homes, and in-home care.

"I have shared that information with my siblings, with interesting results. My sister has made it quite clear that she would not permit Dad to live in a nursing home unless he did not have the mental acumen to know where he was or needed twenty-four-hour nursing supervision,

"I also know that Dad is aware of home-care options because when my mother was ill, before she died, she used a very good home-care service. A homemaker from that service still visits Dad daily to fix his evening meal, except on weekends."

David is fortunate. He has not been faced with the need to make critical decisions on short notice in a strange environment. His advice to others is to do "homework" before the situation reaches a crisis stage.

The die is cast. How we handle it is the question at hand. If we are awake and aware, if we do a little thinking ahead of time, if we find opportunities to discuss the matter with the person or persons affected most directly, the situation often can be resolved positively, with little rancor, fear, and disruption.

But to let the matter go, to ignore it as if it will not happen to us, is to court emotional, financial, and possibly physical problems for family and patient. These problems will be much harder to deal with after the fact.

Part of the purpose of this book is to provide guidelines for people in need of home health care. But there are other books that will do this very well.

Another reason for writing this book is to alert people to the need to begin planning ahead for the time when they or an elder loved one may need care. There is no need for you to duplicate the problems presented throughout the book.

But our principal reason for writing this book is to try to make our nation more aware of the increasing problems that have to be confronted by us if we are to maintain a quality of life throughout our golden years.

KARLA

A responsible, well-organized woman, Karla, over the years, had accumulated an incredible array of antiques and small jeweled items, which she had displayed in her home. The back of a sofa was strewn with ropes and strands of pearls. Glass cabinets held hundreds of pieces of jewelry.

In her late eighties and weighing just over eighty pounds, Karla had a housekeeper and a gardener. As she grew older, and with no immediate family, Karla obtained a conservator for her estate and planned her will and the disposition of her collection.

When we were called in, Karla had suffered some medical problems, had been hospitalized, and now was ready to go home with twenty-four-hour care. The conservator had asked the doctor for recommendations. He suggested a homemaker he knew. But the conservator also realized, much to his credit, that Karla needed additional care that only someone with nursing skills could provide.

We began providing private duty care. Within a few weeks, the nurses were reporting back that things around the house were missing. Karla didn't think it was her trusted housekeeper or gardener, who had been with her for twenty years, so that meant it had to be either the nurses or the homemaker supplied by the doctor.

The conservator was very responsible. He called us, explained the situation, and stated that he had hired a private investigator. He said frankly that the three nurses we referred were suspect, as was the homemaker, but that the homemaker came with references and her husband was a minister.

We believed in our people. They had been checked out and had proven themselves on other occasions.

The detective visited the homemaker in her home. He quickly realized that there were a number of things in the house that just weren't congruent with the earnings level of the homemaker and her minister husband. When questioned about several items, the minister said they had been fortunate to receive a number of gifts over the years from friends and parishioners.

But the detective, not believing the story, took the minister's bible and asked the wife to swear on the bible that her story was true. The woman broke down and ultimately admitted that she had taken the items.

A few days later, when one of the nurses was leaving Karla's house at the end of her shift, she discovered a paper shopping bag on the porch. Inside were the missing items. All had been previously catalogued, appraised, and donated to the Smithsonian Museum, to be delivered upon Karla's death. The value, it turned out, was over $100,000.

2. Comes the Revolution

As Americans, when we hear the term *revolution* we tend to think of an uprising in some small South American nation, the Soviet Revolution of 1917, or the French Revolution, the date of which most of us have long since forgotten if, indeed, we ever knew.

We may be surprised then to learn that the United States is in the midst of a major revolution costing more than many nations generate in annual gross national product and involving virtually every citizen.

It is a health care revolution.

Former Secretary of Health, Education, and Welfare in the Carter Administration Joseph A. Califano, Jr., has written eloquently and convincingly about it in his book *America's Health Care Revolution.*

Former Colorado Governor Richard Lamm has also recognized the revolution and has proposed some far-reaching and controversial changes in his article, "The Ten Commandments of Health Care," in the May/June 1987 issue of *The Humanist.*

U.S. Senator John Melcher, Chairman, Senate Special Committee on Aging, made this strong statement in the spring of 1987. "It's our responsibility to help the elderly and the sick. We have to offer reasonable alternatives to the high cost of hospitals and nursing homes. And that means home care. But not the kind of home care in which patients are ignored, physically abused, and robbed. No, I'm talking about a type of home care that provides attentive care, nutrition, and transportation and a number of other services for those who depend upon home-care aides."

And the late Congressman Claude Pepper, chairman of the House Subcommittee on Health and Long-Term Care, issued numerous reports on the nation's health-care system, citing startling facts and urging immediate action to stave off the long-term effects of the system's abuse.

The term *revolution*, as defined by Webster, means "a sudden, radical, or complete change" and "activity or movement designed to effect fundamental changes." That is just what is happening in our health-care system in the United States. It is occurring in our state and federal legislative bodies, it is occurring among our citizens and it is just beginning.

Let us be more specific and more to the point as it relates to home health care.

Secretary Califano notes, "The revolutionary forces at work are profound. In science, our genius for invention is serving up incredible diagnostic, surgical, and biomedical breakthroughs that blur the lines between life and death and hold the promise of remarkable cures and the threat of unacceptable costs.

"In demography, the graying of America presents a burgeoning population of elderly citizens who consume the most expensive high-tech medicine and who already strain our capacity to provide adequate medical, nursing home, and home care.

"In law and religion, our judges, ethicists, and moral theologians are confounded by the Pandora's box of medical discoveries that insist they reexamine questions as fundamental as when life begins and ends."

Califano goes on to state that perceived and real waste and inefficiency are forcing social and cultural changes in how we see the health-care system and its purveyors and in how we perceive our own responsibilities in this system.

We believe Califano's call for awareness is not only important, but vital to our well being as a nation. We believe we must educate ourselves as to the realities of how decisions are being made by physicians and hospitals, decisions which directly affect our health and well-being.

We believe we must speak out on the need to find ways to cut costs and to assist us—all of us—in finding ways to prevent hospitalization.

And we believe we must speak up about the needs to provide people in need with health care within their homes and to provide caregivers who are trained, monitored, and appropriate for the needs of the individual.

One of the indisputable facts of the health-care revolution in the United States is that we are living longer and, because of the baby boomers, there soon will be more of us living longer . . . and making demands on our health-care system such as have never before existed.

The answer, which has become increasingly clear, is not just to accept that age will cause people to need and use hospitals and nursing homes as they have in the past several decades. For one thing, the costs of these will be too high for most of us. For another, there will not be enough facilities to care for all of us if we continue to deal with health-care problems as we have in the past. And, finally, we are a generation of individuals that has been pursuing a quality of life. We believe everyone wants to maintain that quality throughout their lifetime, and several years in a nursing home is not a promising prospect.

Again we cite Califano; "We have the most advanced medical technology on this earth, elaborately equipped medical schools, regional cancer centers that are the envy of capitals of the civilized world, and an abundance of superb specialists and hospitals.

"But the soaring cost of health care threatens to deny even the affluent access to the miracles we have come to expect, and the billions we've spent have not given millions of uninsured Americans basic health care."

Let's look a little closer at the realities of the health care revolution, how it got to the point of revolution, and what it means to each of us.

THE EVOLUTION OF HEALTH CARE IN AMERICA

According to a report by Congressman Pepper's subcommittee, the origins of our American health care system go back to the late 1800s, when, interestingly enough, a severe shortage of physicians in the country demanded that nurses and volunteers be pressed into service to serve the needs of the ill in their homes. In-home health care was in vogue even then.

"In-home health agencies thus were born in crisis, their primary purpose being to bring the rudiments of modern health care to those who could not integrate with the mainstream of American medicine. Nurses and volunteers sought out needy people in their respective residences and cared for them there," the subcommittee report states.

Over the years, Congress began to expand the meager health-care services the federal government provided the people. In the early 1900s, the Public Health Service was instructed to begin the study of infectious diseases and the control of epidemics.

The first governmental health institute, the National Cancer Institute, was established in 1937.

It was not until World War II, however, that substantial investments were made in health-care training and medical research. In the years between 1944 and 1984, the National Institutes of Health were founded to deal with diseases of the eye, mental health, kidney disorders, heart, lungs and blood, neurological matters, alcoholism, and drug abuse.

Major concerns about health care were expressed by Presidents Franklin D. Roosevelt, Harry S Truman, John F. Kennedy, and Lyndon B. Johnson, and each proposed major legislation that advanced the cause of health care in the nation. Truman proposed the first sweeping health insurance program in 1945 and promptly met with opposition from the American Medical Association, which branded it as a step toward socialized medicine; some even considered the proposal a communist idea.

In 1964, the Hill-Burton Act passed Congress and provided for the construction of hospitals across the nation, particularly in low-income states.

The 1960s saw significant changes in the government's role in the health-care field as Congress passed the Kerr-Mills bill to provide the states with funds to guarantee medical assistance for the elderly.

It further saw both Presidents Kennedy and Johnson proposing sweeping health-care legislation. Kennedy's untimely death was credited by some as providing added impetus to Johnson's efforts to persuade Congress to pass such legislation, and Medicare and Medicaid were passed in 1965.

That same year, Johnson succeeded in getting passed a bill referred to as the Heart Disease, Cancer, and Stroke Bill, which provided for regional medical centers across the nation, to focus on these problems.

Although the Medicare and Medicaid programs have been modified from time to time, little of significance was done to change them until the early 1980s when a program was instituted that severely affected critical-care hospitals. This program, which developed specific reimbursable fees for certain services, meant that hospitals could no longer keep patients in expensive beds beyond a certain number of days. Nor could they charge beyond certain established norms for various hospital services. The result was that many patients went home or to convalescent hospitals or nursing homes "quicker and sicker."

Also in the early '80s came a proliferation of for-profit in-home health-care agencies. The result of sending people home earlier from hospitals was that there were more people who needed in-home health care.

The health-care system had come full circle. Once again nurses and caregivers were going into people's homes to provide needed services. However,

Congress made only modest provisions for Medicare or Medicaid coverage for this kind of service. Thus, while people avoided expensive hospital costs, mostly covered by Medicare, they were incurring new costs, albeit less expensive, required for needed in-home care. And they were finding that these costs were out-of-pocket, meaning they were not covered by Medicare or their private insurance plans!

WHO CARES?

Many people care. Those who need the care and can't pay for it. Those who have meager resources that would be depleted in a matter of months. The families of most of these people care. The generation of young men and women in their thirties and forties care because they can see themselves having to provide for the needs of elderly parents while, at the same time, putting their children through college. Liberals and conservatives care because eventually the need for in-home care for persons afflicted by mental or physical infirmities will affect all of us.

Indeed, the Heritage Foundation, a conservative think tank in Washington, has observed in its 1984 publication, *Mandate for Leadership: II*, "The keystone of long-term health care policy should be a comprehensive program fostering home care services."

Secretary Califano, a liberal by almost anyone's standards, agrees. He states in an article in *50 Plus* magazine, "I think we have to provide the ability for people to stay at home, to grow old at home, to die at home, if they so choose. We have to start paying for home health care in a big way in this country. In the short run, it may cost a little bit more, but in the long run it will save a lot of money."

New York Governor Mario Cuomo notes, "At no time in history have the challenges of providing health care been so great. With rising medical costs and tight controls on utilization of hospital beds and services, home health care agencies have gained new stature as an integral part of the health care delivery system."

It seems we all agree. Or do we? Who opposes home health care?

It is difficult and perhaps unfair to point fingers at any one or several individuals and say, "They oppose home health care." But there are people who, because of their particular vantage point, because of how they look at the issue, because of the jobs they hold or the regulations they are required to enforce, have placed roadblocks in the path of development of a meaningful home health-care system.

Pepper's report states that " . . . home health care has become the most regulated of American industries. At a time when the airlines, the trucking industry, hospitals, and nursing homes are being deregulated, the Department of Health and Human Services has promulgated an oppressive series of requirements applicable to home health agencies."

The congressman and his subcommittee continue: "The contention of this report is that the administrative restrictions placed on home care providers are punitive. They are designed to restrict the statutory Medicare benefit, to force providers out of business, or to force them to subsidize Medicare with revenues raised from . . . Medicare patients."

What then is not covered? Are not millions of people benefiting from Medicare and Medicaid? Who are these people who are apparently falling through the cracks?

They are people like you and like me, simply selected by fate to be among those who suffer from one form of chronic ill health or another. Consider the following:

The Pepper report states that in 1979–80, about 2.7 million older persons living in their communities needed the assistance of another person to perform one or more selected personal care or home management activities.

"Selected personal care activities," the report stated, "included bathing, dressing, eating, getting in or out of a bed or chair, or caring for a bowel-control device.

"Selected home management activities included walking or going outside, preparing meals, routine chores, shopping, or handling money.

"Persons classified as needing assistance were those who need help from another person to do one or more of these activities, could not do one or more of them at all, or stayed in bed most or all of the time."

JOANNE

Joanne is a pleasant, plump, soft-spoken woman in her forties. She is also a diabetic and, as a result, is legally blind. She told the following story to the House Subcommittee on Health and Long-Term Care in March 1986.

"I am a diabetic. This condition caused renal (kidney) failure and I must have dialysis treatment three days a week. In January 1985, I had an operation to place a fistula in my arm for dialysis treatment. After the surgery, I developed reduced functions in my right arm and movement of my fingers and thumb was impaired. While in the hospital, I also suffered a stroke, which caused further weakness in my right arm. In addition to the renal failure, the diabetes has caused retinopathy, leaving me legally blind.

"When I was discharged from the hospital in January 1985, I was very weak. I required help with all the daily necessities of living, including bathing, dressing, transferring, and meal preparation. I was referred to the visiting-nurse service at this time. Physical therapists and occupational therapists worked with me to help me regain my dexterity and strength. The therapy was successful in that I can now walk a few feet using a walker.

"Nursing visits were ordered to make sure that a capable person was giving me daily insulin shots. Home health aides visited to help with my personal care. Reimbursements for these necessities from health visits were subsequently denied . . . on the basis that I am not homebound.

"The determination of my homebound status did not seem justified. I only leave my home three times a week for my dialysis treatments. This is a life-saving procedure, not a leisure-time activity.

"Following the denial I requested a reevaluation. I have recently been notified that the . . . physical and occupational therapists will be paid. However, a denial of the nursing and home health aides would not be revised because my diabetic condition existed for many years. Before my January 1985 hospitalization, I was independent on insulin administration. After the surgery, I was not able to self-administer the insulin and nursing visits were necessary. . . . "

Ask yourself; Should Joanne have qualified? Ask yourself; What were her alternatives? What would you have done in the same situation?

Another individual, Randy, testified that she has cystic fibrosis, a condition where mucus builds up in the lungs to the point where the individual has enormous trouble breathing. There are 47 million people with chronic lung diseases in the United States.

Currently eligible for Medicare, Randy was forced to use the outpatient department of her local hospital for treatment. The cost of these treatments was $190 a day. The same treatment at home would have cost sixty dollars a day.

Randy pointed out that it would save the government a lot of money if the same treatment could have been administered at her home.

The necessity of obtaining treatment at the hospital also causes physical difficulty for Randy, requiring her to be up at a very early hour to go through a lengthy preparation just to go out. And, of course, there was the added and unreimbursable expense of transportation to and from the hospital.

HOME CARE NEEDED BY ONE IN SEVEN

According to figures compiled by the National Association of Home Care in Washington, DC, one out of every seven Americans, or forty million people, were in need of home health care in 1986. Yet only about 2 million people benefited.

The files of the NAHC are filled with stories of people who needed care and were denied it, of people who were adjudged by some bureaucrat to be ineligible because:

- the individual was considered too sick;
- the individual wasn't sick enough to qualify for skilled nursing care;
- the individual wasn't considered homebound;
- the individual's care wasn't considered reasonable and necessary and ordered by a physician.

Those are the rules. At the same time, according to the NAHC, there has been a 37 percent increase in the number of people going into home care since the tighter regulations governing hospital reimbursement forced people to go home quicker and sicker.

Consider the testimony of Val Halamandaris, Esq., president of the National Association for Home Care and a former House and Senate aide, before Congressman Pepper's subcommittee in March 1986. ". . . Home health agencies are the safety net that we, all of us, put underneath to catch people coming out of hospitals. The idea is that we can move people out of hospitals into less expensive levels of care. The idea is now that we have saved billions of dollars by moving people out of hospitals earlier (we have reduced the average length of stay that Medicare is paying for by over two days for every Medicare beneficiary) that we should allocate some few nickels or some few millions of dollars to take care of those individuals at home.

"What this government has done, unfortunately, is to try to trim the candle at both ends. Having saved billions of dollars by moving people out of the hospital earlier, we have failed to expand, even by a small amount, the dollars to pay for home care.

"We have saved billions of dollars and, at the same time, we have increasingly proved or found ineligible people who need home health care.

"It is central to not only the oldest people of this country, but to 31 million Americans. There are at this time, 10 million children who are in hospitals day in and day out who could be cared for at home.

"There are millions of disabled individuals . . . who have been in accidents who could be cared for at home for a fraction of the cost of storing them in institutions or simply ignoring and abandoning them, and the cost to society is massive.

"When will America wake up? When will America see that we have at our fingertips the solution for a problem that has haunted all of us, the solution of catastrophic health protection based on home health care."

The answer, the report suggests, is citizen action. "Unless an aroused public and the Congress intervene, the result will be a sharp decrease in the limited home care benefits now available under Medicare rather than the extension of these services to the 5.5 million Americans who currently need such care and are going without it."

And, we might add, the millions more who are paying for it themselves, but exhausting their savings and those of their families in the process.

History, we are told, tends to repeat itself. And

35

the cause of most citizen revolutions has not been philosophy or greed or power. It has been human suffering. It has been to provide for the basics in our lives; food, shelter, work, and—now—health care.

What we are seeing today is not a revolution in the classic sense of the word, but a revolution nevertheless. Citizens are becoming aware and will continue to recognize the growing need, in this the wealthiest of all nations, for adequate health care for our people. And for development of options that will provide for a better quality of living throughout our life.

FRANCINE

At one time a highly skilled and regionally acclaimed painter, Francine had graduated from a top Eastern women's college and had studied art at the University of California. She was bright, outgoing, and, as was often the case with artists in the '20s and '30s, somewhat bohemian in her lifestyle; what one might call counterculture today.

Francine had been instrumental in developing an art alliance in her small artists' oceanfront community. She was well liked, well known, and respected. The Francine we met, then in her midseventies, did not resemble the Francine we just described. We found a thin, filthy, stringy, wiry-haired creature with wild eyes who might have been cast in a horror film.

Worse still, Francine was forced to reside in a tiny, dingy, cluttered attic-like room in her own home, while her son and his girl friend occupied the downstairs and lived in a hazy, drug-induced stupor.

It was hard to believe this was the same, once proud, active, talented woman we had heard about years earlier. But a few of her paintings hung around the tiny house, providing a few touches of life and color and reminders of her past.

We had received an emergency call from the son. At the time, he had been calling names from ads in the newspaper and most respondents, after one look at the situation, left and did not return. He was finding it virtually impossible to obtain care for his mother and unwilling to provide it himself.

We discovered Francine lying in a bed soaked through from urine, completely unable to get out of bed and to the bathroom.

Her hair was twisted and tangled; most of her teeth were missing. The room smelled almost to the point of making one ill. The clutter and debris made it difficult to get to Francine, let alone for her to get out of bed and maneuver across the upper floor of the house.

If Francine had had an emergency, there was no way she could have communicated with the son downstairs.

When questioned, the son admitted his mother had been isolated upstairs for about three months and that he had not made any personal effort to change her sheets, see that she had a bath, or provide personal care. "Am I supposed to do that?" he asked.

Francine was totally disoriented and could not communicate. She was not responsive to various forms of stimulation. Her medicine cabinet had bottles dating back to 1957. She had no clothes whatsoever. She was like an unhappy animal, alternately whining and weepy. Once cleaned, she appeared a lot happier and even smiled.

The son seemed totally detached, as if the problem was someone else's. He appeared unable to evaluate the problem and take action, largely devoid of common sense, dulled by drugs.

We enlisted a doctor to evaluate her condition. The doctor's diagnosis was senile dementia. With a clean environment, someone to assist her in getting up and around, the quality of her life could have been improved substantially. However, with no responsible family member, no prearranged conservator, she was placed in a nursing home. Francine, alone, died several months later.

and services, but are not usually familiar with the pros and cons of each. They can provide what information they may have on each, including addresses and phone numbers and a person to contact.

They frequently do not know which are highly responsive and which are not; which perform needs assessments, and which simply provide an individual to do a job; which have a high preponderance of people who are trained and certified, licensed, and registered; which are bonded and which are not; which are qualified to assist with the processing of Medicare and other insurance forms.

Be wary of hospitals with their own agency. They have a vested interest in your business but that does not assure service and performance or quality of care. Ask the same questions of them and monitor their performance and costs as you would any other care deliverer.

Another logical source of information is your local Alliance on Aging office. In some parts of the country this organization may be listed under a different name, but in virtually every city and county there is an agency that deals with the problems of the aging.

There may also be a heading in the yellow pages of your phone directory called Senior Citizens' Service Organizations. These organizations deal regularly with problems of the aging and may be able to make knowledgeable recommendations. But don't count on it. Logical or not, these organizations usually have no specialty, but a range of information, and may not be able to do anything more than to provide you with brochures and refer you to someone else.

When contacting in-home care agencies directly,

there are several things to be taken into consideration.

Because each person requiring in-home health-care assistance has individual needs—and if you are planning well in advance of the time when you or a loved one is likely to need this service—you should ask about the scope of services provided.

You will want to know how many people they have on staff or on call, what geographical areas they serve, how they monitor the work of their people, whether administrators and supervisors are registered nurses or other professionals who can spot problems which are medically related, whether they will meet with you and/or the person in need prior to providing services, whether they will work with your doctor. You should ask whether help is available twenty-four hours a day and on weekends and holidays or whether it is more limited. And, of course, they should be willing to discuss costs with you and tell you directly what would and what would not be covered by Medicare and other insurance plans.

CAREGIVER LEVELS

Inquire whether the agency or service has various levels of caregiver—from those who can provide routine living assistance such as dressing and getting meals, shopping and getting to the doctor, to registered nurses who can provide more sophisticated medical services. Many provide a full range of services.

Unfortunately, not all states have uniform regulations regarding training and certification of home health aides. California, one of the more progressive in this regard, requires certain levels of competency, education, and training for registered nurses, another level for licensed vocational nurses (sometimes referred to elsewhere as licensed practical nurses), and a third level for certified nurses' assistants.

Certified nurses' assistants may be used by some services and agencies as in-home personal care aides, while other services and agencies require little or no training and no certification for the same services.

We believe, because most in-home personal care needs are created as a result of some physical or mental infirmity, it is important, wherever possible, to use certified nurses' assistants or persons who have some formal training for such personal care activities as bathing, getting in and out of bed, walking any distance, and other personal care needs. If the need for care has been created by a mental or physical infirmity, it is important, in our judgment, that the caregiver be able to spot potential danger signs and indications that an individual may be in need of additional medical attention; enough so that he or she can call attention to the matter.

There is a major and important difference between a caretaker and a caregiver. We have seen too many instances where a companion or caretaker has not recognized a slight stroke, improper medicinal intake, improper changing of bandages, or other problems.

DARLENE

Darlene was one of our more unusual cases. An

avid swimmer, she had suffered a ruptured aorta while swimming at a local pool. She had been pulled from the water and flown by helicopter to a hospital some one hundred miles distant in an emergency rescue operation.

As a result, she was paralyzed from the waist down. Gradually, she worked her way back to the point where, with the assistance of friends, a variety of community resources, and a motorized cart, she could get around and even resume swimming.

Several months later, Darlene, a smoker, had fallen asleep in bed and had set the bed clothing on fire. Because she had no feeling in her extremities, the fire began to eat away at one leg without her knowing it. It was her dog who finally aroused her and alerted her neighbors, but not before the leg was badly burned. The leg had to be amputated below the knee.

Darlene then redirected her focus away from herself to her animals and gradually became angry, ornery, and difficult for our caregivers to deal with.

Following this episode, she had a variety of needs, including specialized nutritional requirements, but she resisted our nursing care. She hired homemakers who prepared incorrect foods, could not deal with her increasing depression, and then didn't show up for work. Her mental condition worsened. Darlene shifted her attention to her animals. She used her limited funds to hire a driver to take her dogs to the groomer for a perm.

Eventually Darlene could no longer pay the bills. Ultimately, her family arrived from the Midwest and assumed responsibility for her care.

Darlene used help obtained from the newspapers or friends. The complexity of her situation after the ruptured aorta required attention that could not have been adequately supplied by people without some nursing skills. We believe she very likely would have avoided physical and mental complications had she had adequate and informed care. This case highlights the need for states to provide for standards of care that would assure caregivers be of at least a minimal competency level. In California, the certified nurses' assistant program consists of approximately 150 classroom hours and 50 clinical hours, which, in night-time classes, ranges from three to six months of training, at a cost of approximately five dollars plus the price of manuals.

NONMEDICAL PROBLEMS

Just because an individual has recovered from an illness does not mean he or she no longer requires attention or resources to continue living a meaningful life.

Many elderly people languish in rooms, apartments, or homes alone and without necessary and beneficial services; services that are available to them at little or no cost and which, when utilized, could significantly enrich the quality of their lives.

A sample of services that are developing out of the ever-increasing need for elderly care are:

Making informed decisions
In-home care
Nursing home care
Medicare

Medi-Cal (in California)
Supplemental Security Income

Alternatives for managing personal or financial matters

Advocacy
Counseling
Day care
Education
Emergencies
Employment
Finances
Food and meal programs
Services for the handicapped
Health
Housing
Legal services
Transportation
Visitor program
Volunteer organization

More specific services and specializations are:

Alcoholism
Alzheimer's disease and related disorders
Cancer, diabetes, heart and lung disease organizations
Domestic crisis service
Eyecare hotline
Food stamps
Hospice
Lawyers' referral service
Meals on Wheels

Telephone Lifeline Service
Senior Companion Program
Women's Crisis Service
Victims of Crimes

In each case, help may be just a phone call away.

An important area of care that has been overlooked until very recently is elder abuse. Elderly people, more than any other age group except children, often because of physical and mental debilitation, are more likely to suffer abuse at the hands not only of strangers, but often and unfortunately, family and friends.

Many elderly people are extremely vulnerable because they need and generally want love and attention and they often are alone and distant from children who may live in other parts of the state or nation. As such, they are highly susceptible to physical, emotional, psychological, and financial abuse and neglect.

ESTHER

Esther lived in a handsome condominium, part of an expensive complex nestled in one of the most beautiful small valleys in California. The complex sits by a championship golf course at the base of a small mountain range and, with a view across the valley, the beauty is breathtaking.

Esther's condominium was owned by her son and, conveniently enough, was adjacent to the one in which her son and daughter-in-law lived. The son, a wealthy man involved with the film industry, spent most of the week away on business.

49

It sounds pleasant enough on the surface, yet Esther was a victim of neglect and psychological abuse. The daughter-in-law refused to have anything to do with Esther. Although Esther could have used the human contact and attention, the daughter-in-law, with the full knowledge of the son, had little more than cursory contact with her mother-in-law. Food was prepared and brought into the apartment and left on a tray. Meals were not eaten together. Esther did not drive and thus had no way of getting out into the community. She did not have a phone or friends in the area whom she could call or who would come and see her.

One day we received a call from Esther's doctor inquiring if we had a nurse who could call on her patient. We did. When we arrived, we found the woman lying on a filthy bed covered with feces, after multiple bouts with diarrhea. Although there was a bathroom nearby, Esther, because she was a stroke victim, had been unable to get to it.

The daughter-in-law was probably aware of the situation, but was incapable of handling it. A housekeeper hired by the daughter-in-law came occasionally and arrived while we were there. She, too, was astonished to find Esther in this condition and was unprepared to deal with her.

After we cleaned Esther and changed her linens, we called her doctor and asked about Esther's medical background. The doctor admitted she had not seen Esther personally, but the son had called, seeking her help. She, in turn, called us.

The daughter-in-law refused to talk to us and to do anything to aid her mother-in-law. The doctor, after our report, did visit Esther and explained to the son and daughter-in-law the need for care.

Esther subsequently was put in a convalescent hospital and the son and daughter-in-law moved from the area.

Our files and those of the state and county are full of stories like this. The abuse of our elderly spares no one. The cases include rich and poor, people of all races and social strata. At least in California, there are phone numbers to call and report elder abuse where action will be taken. And for every case of abuse or neglect reported, there are countless more that never are revealed, which people are reluctant or afraid to report.

WHAT CONSTITUTES ABUSE?

Many things constitute abuse. Included among them are: direct physical harm; lack of food; lack of medical care; overmedication; sexual exploitation; neglect; verbal threats; creation of fear; isolation; withholding of emotional support; theft; fraud; misuse of funds or property; extortion; duress; coercion; locking someone up; forced removal from the home or forced entry into the home; denial of food, clothing, shelter, or health care.

WHAT ARE THE SYMPTOMS OF ABUSE?

Symptoms vary according to the category: physical, emotional, or psychological; financial or material; civil rights and denial of basic needs.

They range from such obvious things as cuts,

bruises, and welts that appear with regularity, often old and new at the same time, poor hygiene, absent patches of hair, burns, soiled clothing or bedding, hidden injuries or bruises, unusual and regular use of the emergency room of the hospital, and improper level of in-home care or supervision.

Evidence of psychological or emotional problems include: depression, unusual deference, passivity, fearfulness, hopelessness, reluctance to talk openly, denial, agitation, trembling, confusion and distortion, habit disorders, and lack of responsiveness.

Financial abuse might occur with: unusual activity in bank accounts or with credit cards; recent acquaintances expressing unusual affection for the elderly wealthy; unusual interest by a caregiver in person's financial affairs; the caregiver has no obvious means of support; the caregiver tries to isolate the person from friends and family, thereby generating overreliance on the caregiver.

Rights violations may include: person being locked in the home or a room, interception of visitors and/or mail, elimination of phone, a person being forced to do things against his/her will. Abuse is often unintentional.

MILTON AND EVA

Milton and Eva had spent their lives in the movie colony and now, in their eighties, were retired. Their little house was bursting at the seams, not only with a lifetime of accumulations, but with what appeared to be years of debris that should have gone out with the trash. The yard was a junk collector's dream.

52

Milt, a bulky six-feet-four, was clearly an alcoholic. His days were occupied by three things: drinking, taking care of his wife, who had broken her hip and recently had been discharged from the hospital, and, as it turned out, in filing lawsuits against virtually everyone.

No matter who we sent to care for his wife, the person was unacceptable to Milt. Further, he sought to have our caregivers do tasks around the house and yard and pay attention to him and his wishes rather than attend to his wife. He was verbally abusive when they declined. At the same time, his wife, a short, rotund woman, required regular attention due to her size, inability to move, and periodic incontinence.

We finally had to call Adult Protective Services. They confirmed that Milt was unintentionally abusing his wife by denying her adequate care. This undoubtedly was caused by his drinking, which caused him to lose touch with reality and with the plight of his wife.

We believe Milt loved his wife; they had been married fifty years. But his intentions were impeded by alcoholism and, as a result, she suffered.

WHAT CAN BE DONE?

Our position is that help—whatever is needed—truly is just a phone call away. It simply requires that someone care enough to call for help.

If you know of someone who has been subject to abuse or neglect, you can contact an elder abuse program, your local police department, or the state attorney general's office and receive information and counseling on what constitutes abuse, how can you document it, how to report it, and what will be done about it. In most states, local law-enforcement agencies are both knowledgeable and sympathetic to elder abuse and will work with you to correct it. Confidentiality is adhered to.

We also believe that you or your loved one must acquaint yourselves well ahead of time with services that are available to help prevent elder abuse. There is no substitute for advance planning and knowledge.

One way to lessen the chances of abuse and neglect is to have enough people around to prevent isolation and to assure that unusual situations and the symptoms described above are recognized by someone. Isolation of the individual helps to promote and hide abuse.

If your city or county has offices on the aging, call them. Visit a senior citizens' center and see what resources they have. Perhaps a Meals on Wheels Program or a Friendly Visitor Program would be beneficial.

In many areas you will find such services as Friendly Visitor, someone who contacts an elderly individual through personal visits or phone calls on a regular basis to show that someone cares and to reassure them.

In many areas, a senior day center, where seniors can get out of the house on their own and take advantage of hot meals served at noon in a communal setting, is available. This provides an opportunity for socialization as well as nutrition.

When people are shut in, unable to get out on their own or without help, a Meals on Wheels Program may deliver hot meals to the house.

Know what services are available; what options

you or your loved one have.

If health care is the most important consideration for you or a loved one, visit in-home health agencies and services. Inspect nursing homes and
residential care facilities. Become a member of the
American Association of Retired Persons and send for
their free material on these subjects. Become a
knowledgeable, educated citizen. Even if you have
never considered yourself a community activist, find
out what is going on in your community as it relates
to elder care and services.

The point we are trying to make here is that it is
our responsibility to know resources are available, to
develop resources that are not in our community,
and to evaluate them in light of our needs or those of
loved ones.

Our cities, counties, states, and our federal
government are beginning to provide a variety of help
programs of which we can take advantage—for both
information and practical assistance. We urge you to
take full advantage of them. Your tax dollars support
them.

HARRY

Harry lived with Jonas, his lover of some forty
years. They were in the antique business and their
handsome home was filled with attractive items from
throughout the world. They lived in sophisticated
luxury.

Harry developed a number of physical problems
that started with congestive heart failure, aggravated
by an unintentional drug overdose and depression

about the prospect of losing his lifestyle. He had to be hospitalized.

Upon his discharge, the doctor prescribed in-home care for Harry. Jonas resisted. Two elderly people, we have discovered, often become protective of each other and of their privacy. Harry and Jonas were no exception.

The alternative to in-home care was to send Harry to a convalescent home, a course again rejected by both men. Faced with no other options, they finally agreed to in-home care.

In-home care presented other problems. First, they did not want female nurses. Male nurses are not in abundant supply and, when we did supply male nurses, Jonas became jealous and abusive, making it difficult for them to appropriately care for Harry. Second, each resented and fussed about the attention the other was receiving. When one liked a nurse, the other didn't. One wanted a gourmet cook, not a nurse. They argued and bickered with each other constantly.

Harry and Jonas had many visitors coming in and out of their home, mainly young men. Our nurses began reporting that some of the expensive items in the home had begun to disappear. When visitors were present, they might be found unsupervised anywhere in the house. We believed the visitors were taking advantage of Harry and Jonas.

The two provided a classic denial case. They refused to admit they were getting older. They tried to maintain a youthful approach to their lives while bickering like an old married couple. They were not easy to be around.

Our nurses found them inflexible and unwilling

to adopt a new lifestyle more conducive to their age and health situation. They could not adapt to change, as is the case with many older people.

They were uncooperative with our nurses, as well as with nurses from other agencies, after we declined to provide care any longer. They were also uncooperative with their attorney and unwilling to restrict access of questionable visitors to their home. As a result, their health declined rapidly, they continued to lose items from their home and they were manipulated by a host of guests who found them easy prey.

Harry died within a year and Jonas shortly thereafter.

4. Caveat Emptor

Caveat emptor—Let the buyer beware. For many years this was the philosophy under which America's economic system operated. The provider of goods and services was not required to give warranties or guarantees to the buyer. It was, in effect, the buyer's responsibility to be astute enough to know whether the seller's claims were valid and whether the buyer would receive value in return for his money.

Fortunately, in large measure, that situation has changed today. Most purveyors of goods and services are required by various laws to provide the buyer with certain warranties and guarantees that the product or service is as represented.

A notable exception is the services provided by physicians, attorneys, accountants, the courts, and guardians or conservators of an individual's personal and financial affairs.

While not intending to impugn the motivations of these valuable professionals, it is nevertheless a fact that these people can and do provide services that most of us take at face value and seldom challenge.

Equally disquieting is the situation where a well-meaning but uninformed relative or friend seeks help for an individual and, in the process, makes poor and ill-advised decisions.

GUARDIANSHIPS

A classic example, though not one we find frequently, is the circumstance that creates a guardianship. Shocking as it may seem, the right to hire an attorney, to vote, to drive a car, to decide where one will live and to handle one's own financial affairs can be—and frequently is—taken away from an elderly person, without that person's acquiescence and sometimes without the individual's knowledge.

Frequently the responsibility for administering to the needs of an elderly and often ill person will be assigned by the court to a relative or friend with the belief that someone else will act in the best interest of the individual who, the court decides, needs assistance. And often the person assigned is woefully unresponsive or ill equipped to assume the responsibility.

How does this situation come about? When a friend or family member, a doctor, hospital official, attorney, or accountant perceives a situation in which an individual—in the eyes of the person making the decision—can no longer adequately care for him or herself, someone else has to accept the responsibility and assume care of the individual.

If no family member or friend is available or willing, the court is petitioned to appoint a guardian, with no warrantee or guarantee or legal representation in many cases.

In the fall of 1987, the Associated Press wire service carried a lengthy series of articles on guardianships—what they referred to as the last line of protection for the nation's elderly ill—stating that the system is failing those it is designed to protect. Many newspapers across the nation, shocked by the wire service story, conducted their own investigations and ran additional stories with local angles.

The AP story stated, "A yearlong investigation (of the nation's guardianship system) by the Associated Press in courts of all fifty states and the District of Columbia found a dangerously burdened and troubled system that regularly puts elderly lives in the hands of others with little or no evidence of necessity, then fails to guard against theft, abuse and neglect."

The article points out that "elderly in guardianship court are often afforded fewer rights than criminal defendants." It notes that of the 2,200 cases inspected, 44 percent of the time the elderly person was not represented by an attorney, 34 percent of the time the files contained no medical evidence of the person's inability to care for him or herself, and 49 percent of the people were not present at the hearing.

Further, in 48 percent of the cases examined, there was no accounting or only a partial accounting of financial records of the individual, although forty-five of the fifty states require such records be filed regularly.

The potential for mismanagement of the lives and finances of elderly people is huge. The reality, if the AP wire story is to be believed, is already of enormous proportions.

According to the AP survey, the average age of wards in the guardianship cases they examined was age seventy-nine. Two-thirds were female. One-third lived in their own homes before guardianship was imposed. One-third were moved from these homes during guardianship and two-thirds were placed in nursing homes at some point during the guardianship.

In all fairness, it must be noted that a judge approved 97 percent of the petitions for guardianship, but at the same time, only 8 percent of the elderly persons attended the hearings. In only 66 percent of the cases, a physician was consulted.

Although the guardianship program was originally developed to provide protection for elderly people against their being taken advantage of, too often the system breaks down and works against the elderly.

Of particular importance to us, in writing this book, is the health care provided the elderly by the guardian system. The quality of health care unfortunately ties in with the individual's financial well-being. Too often consideration of the latter overrides the former and conservation of funds in an estate becomes more important than conservation of the individual while he or she is alive.

While the AP survey notes that more than 80 percent of the petitions cited health related reasons in requesting guardianship of the elderly person, over one-third of the files examined had no medical information contained within and many more had only sparse information.

Although in theory most states require that files be examined by the court periodically to ascertain that the guardian is providing the court with proper records on both health care and financial status, most court jurisdictions admitted they had neither the staff nor the time or money to monitor files except in the most cursory manner.

We are not saying that guardians or conservators do not provide a valuable service. We are simply saying that an alert individual, concerned with his or her well-being, or that of a loved one, must be alert to potential abuses.

With professionals, "let the buyer beware" is still a warning worth heeding when it comes to your well-being or that of an elderly loved one.

More frequently, we find elderly people themselves choose relatives, friends, or professionals who may have an expertise in one area or another, but usually are ill-equipped to monitor health care needs.

For instance, generally well-meaning, but often one-dimensional attorneys are assigned to take care of an individual's financial needs with the mistaken assumption that this person can provide for a client's personal needs as well.

EMALINE

We first were called by the local hospital to look after Emaline who had fallen a number of times and, after one fall, required hospitalization. Upon her discharge, we were asked to provide care and to do so through her attorney.

The hospital agreed that Emaline was not able to return to her condominium and so we admitted her to our residential care facility. Her mental faculties were clear and she blended in well and seemed happy there.

However, not long thereafter, her attorney moved Emaline back to her condo with the explanation that he had found someone cheaper to care for her at home.

Her attorney had a secretary who has some friends, essentially housekeepers, who did this sort of thing, so the attorney simply referred cases of this kind to his secretary who, in turn, called a friend.

Just three weeks after we learned that Emaline had been readmitted to the hospital after a fall. She had lain in her bathroom for over twenty-four hours before someone found her. We subsequently found out that the attorney, as a cost-savings measure, had cut visits from the caregiver to two times a week.

After several additional falls and hospital stays, Emaline became confused and disoriented. She had suffered a second broken hip and had fractured an elbow. There was no way she would ever be able to function on her own again. She was institutionalized.

In six short months, Emaline lost her physical and mental faculties. We have since discovered that during this critical period, the attorney never once visited her personally. We believe with proper care she would have been able to prolong the quality of her life.

TRUST DEPARTMENTS

For years, individuals with enough funds to require management have looked to bank trust officers for counsel. In most instances, preference surveys have found that bank trust officers are considered more conservative and less speculative in the handling of an individual's funds than a brokerage house. That was their appeal.

The waiting rooms of trust departments frequently were filled with little old ladies and an occasional elderly man making regular visits to see how their fortunes have been doing.

Many men, with investments in stocks, bonds, real estate, and perhaps other areas, believing their wives unable or incapable of managing an estate, put their finances in a trust to be administered by the bank at the time of their death.

And, just as frequently, the bank trust officer found him or herself in a position of making decisions regarding how funds were expended for health-care purposes as well as dealing with tax and real estate situations.

Most trust departments have not traditionally felt comfortable with health-care decisions and frequently have made decisions that were based on financial considerations rather then the level of health care required and the quality of that care.

In recent years, as the number of older people has increased, and the number of firms providing noncritical health care has grown as well, some bank trust officers have chosen to assign the health care of their customers to health-care agencies or, at the least, to hire gerontologists to provide counsel on how to deal with the varied interests of older clients.

In doing so, some have taken the time to become familiar with the various services and options and some have chosen to virtually ignore the situation.

We have made an effort to acquaint bank trust officers with the nature of in-home health care services. Several have welcomed the information and have, in fact, turned the medical care responsibility over to us. We, in turn, keep the trust officer fully informed of our activities on behalf of his client, thereby working as a team.

PAUL

Paul is a trust officer with a large bank with headquarters in a city some distance away. He has a degree of autonomy that many larger trust department people do not. Paul takes action when one of three circumstances occur. In one, a client requests action. In another, a physician requests that a patient receive special care. And third, a family will express concern that they can no longer care for a parent. This is the point when we are called into the picture.

The client and often the family frequently balk at costs. Paul points out the problem of obtaining less qualified and therefore less expensive help. He also points out that when a client hires a homemaker independently, the client assumes responsibility in the same manner as an employer does including supervising, taking over payroll, tax obligations, and workman's compensation. Most clients and families cannot or do not want to handle these responsibilities.

Paul notes that he prefers an intermediary between the client and the caregivers and, for that reason, he uses our service. "This way I'm reasonably assured that the patient will not be robbed blind. Nor that the client will get too dependent upon the caregiver, which could lead to temptation to manipulation and abuse by caregivers."

He also prefers to have a vendor who supplies services rather than an employee. "It is simpler," he adds.

Finally, Paul rightfully observes that it is a trust department's role to manage assets, not to get involved in health care. So hiring a reliable and knowledgeable agency or service is often the answer.

"No one of us is qualified to judge the dispensation of nursing care," Paul states emphatically. "Anyone who says he or she is able is doing the client a disservice."

Hence the emergence of a new type of individual, like Richard, who has become a professional conservator, working independently or for banks or accountants, who manages all aspects of the elderly person's life, and does so for a fee.

RICHARD

A former trust officer at two Western banks, Richard is a soft-spoken, composed man in his early fifties who has a clear commitment to his clients. He began his professional conservatorship when, at the merger of his employer with another bank, he lost his job.

As Richard talked with us, he presented himself in a manner that created confidence—a firm handshake, looking at us directly. He was controlled and knowledgeable, traits that undoubtedly create a level of comfort in his clients.

Richard pointed out that most of his business comes from referrals by attorneys, CPAs, and the retirement community. He feels fortunate that he had been established as a trust officer in the community and the transition to his current business was a smooth one.

Although Richard's work does not require that he be licensed or certified, he noted that if he did not do well by his clients, his referrals would dry up quickly.

Further, if he is a court-appointed conservator, there are records to be maintained for the court and maybe periodic visits by court investigators that help to assure that the client is receiving fair treatment.

In cases where a client's legal, accounting, or medical problems are sufficiently complex, Richard enlists the services of other specialists. He is careful to point out the necessity of not overstepping the realistic bounds of the service he provides.

"I look after the personal and often emotional needs of my clients to a degree that lawyers and trust officers can't or don't," Richard says. "This is a highly personalized business and it takes a great deal of time to obtain the trust of a client and a great deal of patience is often required."

Richard takes charge of his clients' lives at a time when they need security and when they are increasingly less able to make judgments about such things as money management, taxes, and health care.

This type of service is expected to grow in the future and will undoubtedly be staffed in part by trained gerontologists. It remains to be seen whether these people will be licensed and bonded for the protection of the client.

MARCIA

In her heyday, Marcia was a tall, striking, well-groomed, and confident woman. She had successfully raised two fine children, a boy and a girl, and had run a thriving small business.

In her seventies, Marcia's health began to deteriorate. When we first met her, she had fallen and suffered spinal fractures, largely as a result of osteoporosis and arthritis. She also was experiencing the early stages of Parkinson's disease.

When she was ready to be discharged from the hospital, Marcia's son expressed a desire for his mother to receive twenty-four-hour nursing care at home. The doctor complied. Marcia was alert and generally in good spirits, but would be dependent upon nursing care.

The son, believing that his mother's financial affairs would best be managed by a professional, succeeded in having that responsibility transferred to the trust department of his mother's bank.

Not long after, the bank referred the son and daughter to a list of independently hired homemakers who the bank thought might charge lower rates. The family began to hire less expensive and less qualified help. The responsibility for monitoring her care was given by the mother to the daughter. The daughter, an emotional person with no experience in hiring and managing people, made a number of highly questionable decisions.

Marcia's physical and emotional status began to decline. Unnerved by what was happening, concerned over the costs of her mother's care, and believing that something had to be done, the daughter eventually put Marcia into a residential care facility.

Marcia required the attention of a trained caregiver. The residential care facility had none. Within a month, Marcia fell twice, and when her son visited her he found she was suffering from dehydration. On one occasion he discovered she had fallen at night and had lain on the floor for four hours before she was discovered. Overnight care was provided by a housekeeper who spoke little English and whose sole responsibility was to sleep over; simply to be there.

In many states, care homes, by whatever title, usually mandate twenty four-hour coverage, but provide few guidelines as to what type of training or background their employees should have.

In these surroundings, Marcia rapidly lost her will to live and began to slip badly. At this point, our service was contracted to provide needed care to Marcia at the residential facility.

The sad aspect is that none of this need have happened. Properly planned and administered in-home care would have kept Marcia in good health, in good spirits, in her own home, and all at a cost she could afford.

The banker and the daughter were acting from ignorance. The former looked not at the quality of life, but at his fiduciary responsibility. The latter did not explore the options, made emotional rather than rational decisions, and did not look at the level of care her mother would be receiving in the residential care facility. The son refused to step in, even when he saw errors being made. He jeopardized his mother's health because he didn't want to argue with his sister.

We all have a tendency to look at banks, courts, and attorneys as all-knowing and wise advisors. We tend to accept their judgments with little challenge because we question our own knowledge and ability to make sound judgments. Our position is that we all have an obligation to find out the facts, to examine the options, and to question decisions before letting others make them for us or our loved ones.

THE DUTCHMAN

The Dutchman was a delight. A large man, he was expansive in his love of life and of people—gregarious, courtly, giving, loving, and enormously successful. He was used to having his own way without having to resort to being authoritarian and demanding. His charm was infectious and captivating. People close to "Dutch" were loving and loyal in return.

When Dutch's wife died a few years ago, he was disconsolate. In her final months, the wife had around-the-clock nursing care from our service. Dutch elected to keep several of the nurses around for a few weeks during the grief period, paying them well.

Although at age eighty, Dutch was emotionally and physically slipping, his younger brother and his accountant both felt that Dutch should be allowed to continue making his own decisions. "After all, it's his money," they reasoned.

They agreed he needed help at home but looked for more inexpensive care. Our nurses were released. Dutch's accountant hired an attractive, middle-aged woman from an ad in the paper as a live-in companion. The woman quickly became Dutch's protector.

We had become fond of Dutch and, wondering how he was doing, asked our service coordinator to check in on him at one point. During her visit, the coordinator noticed that Dutch was not responding normally. She reported that she suspected he had suffered a mild stroke. The live-in companion did not recognize the symptoms. Dutch was moved to the hospital. When the doctor made his rounds one evening, he found the live-in companion in bed with Dutch.

Shortly thereafter, a police officer arrived at Dutch's home. He was looking for the live-in companion and had a warrant for her arrest. The woman, whom we shall call Beverly, was wanted in Florida for check forgery and dealing in cocaine.

But Dutch had become emotionally and physically dependent on Beverly by now. Despite the fact that Beverly had run up several thousand dollars in charges on Dutch's late wife's credit cards and the discovery that Dutch had provided twenty thousand dollars in cash to Beverly in just a few months, Dutch decided he wanted to keep Beverly in his home. His brother and accountant were unwilling to go against Dutch's wishes.

Dutch hired an attorney to defend Beverly and pay her fines in Florida and she then returned to his home. Shortly thereafter, he suffered another stroke.

Dutch's doctor insisted on regular nursing care, despite Beverly's presence. Dutch required someone to monitor his medicines and, because he was unstable and had begun to fall, he needed someone knowledgeable to help him move around his house.

Still opting to cut costs, the accountant hired homemakers. Before they were discharged, one accepted a ten-thousand-dollar diamond watch and another received several thousand dollars in cash. Both proved to be clever manipulators.

We then received a call from Dutch. He sought our counsel regarding whether he should turn over his financial affairs to his younger brother. We advised he should. However, the brother, living out of town, and feeling the accountant was in control, procrastinated making any decisions.

Recently the situation took a turn for the worse. Beverly convinced Dutch to marry her, took him to the courthouse in a wheelchair, and now his care and his estate are in her control.

We use this story to demonstrate how easily and how often elderly people, especially those who are ill and think of themselves as alone, can be and are manipulated by others.

Both Dutch's brother and his accountant were unwilling to step in and correct an increasingly bad situation because they feared hurting the man who had been so loving and caring and generous to them for so many years. What they lacked was an understanding of what truly is in the individual's best interests. Situations like this are not uncommon.

In our view, it is the responsibility of everyone involved with the individual to stay close to the situation and do everything they can to prevent such manipulative situations from developing and attempt to abort them before it is too late.

To those of us who are approaching the age where we might expect an illness or anticipate the need for help in managing our affairs, we need to select someone trustworthy well in advance, then discuss the situation with them, making it clear what we want and don't want. Finally, both people should thoroughly explore the options that exist to support various circumstances.

Adopt the Boy Scott motto—"Be Prepared!" There is no substitute for preparedness, should we become incapacitated or just need help in managing our affairs.

Look for people—friends, relatives, or others—whom you can trust, who will act responsibly, who have the time and the willingness, and who have the ability to make non-emotional decisions.

Each person should prepare by explaining certain things to the individual chosen to provide the assistance. Among the things that need to be explained are: don't take responsibility for things I can clearly handle; do accept responsibility for those I cannot; accept responsibility to discuss with me any concerns you may have as they arise; check my finances at least quarterly, preferably monthly; require me to make clear why I have made a decision affecting myself, and you should make clear why you are making a decision affecting me; have a thorough understanding of my basic philosophy of life and death and any religious considerations I may have.

Whether dealing with bank trust officers, accountants, lawyers, or court-appointed guardians or conservators, use prudence in overseeing their actions. Do not assume they are flawless and that they will serve all the needs of an elderly loved one or yourself.

While most are well intentioned, and few willfully make decisions that are not in the best interests of their clients, they are human beings who make mistakes in judgment just as you and we do.

Ask questions of these people as they interact with you or your loved ones. Make them explain why they are doing or recommending something. Make certain you understand their actions and, above all, be certain in your own mind that the actions they take are in the best interest of the individual affected.

The point we are trying to make here is that there

is no guarantee or warranty and we, as individuals, cannot rely upon someone else to provide for our loved ones or, in the future, for ourselves. As "buyers" of the services of lawyers, accountants, trust department, guardians—whatever the form—we must be wary.

LUCY

Eighty-two years old, Lucy was an alcoholic whose lifelong battle with the bottle had debilitated her to the point where numerous illnesses now required her to have in-home care. Specifically, she needed assistance with her personal hygiene and transportation to and from doctor's appointments. We were called by her two sons, professional men, one a psychiatrist, both of whom resided some distance away.

Like many elderly ill, Lucy was very lonely and needed the company of others. Yet the sons, who seldom saw her, would only authorize one visit a week for four hours.

When our caregivers arrived after being away for a week, they would find that all the sheets, blankets, towels, pillows from the couch, everything, would be in the bathtub, filled with water.

Lucy would have accidents due to periodic incontinence and her alcoholic condition and, after soiling sheets, pillows, or whatever, she would seek to wash them in the bathtub. But Lucy was unable to wring out the water. Thus, after several days, things began to look and smell highly disagreeable.

The sons would not provide Lucy with a washer

and dryer. We enlisted a laundry service to help with the problem. But we soon found that if our caregiver wasn't right there when the laundry came, Lucy would march out on the porch and drag everything back in and redeposit it in the bathtub.

After weeks, we appealed to the sons to take responsibility for Lucy. We noted that one four-hour visit a week wasn't adequate; it sometimes took almost four hours to get her to disrobe and take a bath. We noted that she needed someone with her in the evening because the problem began at cocktail hour. She needed someone to protect her from herself. We eventually threatened to call Adult Protective Services because we were concerned that she would set herself or the house on fire.

Ultimately, our insistence that Lucy be provided better and more regular care sufficiently irritated the sons that they dropped our service. We have since learned that shortly thereafter, Lucy had several falls while alone in the house and, after one such fall, died.

5. Who, Me?

CLARA

At five-feet-eleven-inches and one hundred and eighty-five pounds, Clara was an imposing figure. She learned early to use size to her advantage, quickly noting that others deferred to her. Size, combined with a quick mind and strong voice, proved to be formidable assets in dealing with others. Clara quickly became both a leader and a forceful advocate of her views on a wide range of subjects. Friends and family alike generally adhered to Clara's wishes.

What worked well for Clara during her youth and middle age began to work to her disadvantage when the first symptoms of Alzheimer's disease began to show. Indeed, the behavior patterns formed through the years proved hard to break as her disease grew worse.

People around Clara simply didn't take charge of the situation and Clara no longer was able. Intimidated as they were when she was well, her friends and family were even more so as her mind began to slip. Clara soon found herself in a never-never land, slipping in and out of lucidity, while people around her did little or nothing.

Fortunately for Clara, a family friend, recognizing the presence of Alzheimer's and the significance of the situation, was able to have the disease diagnosed by a physician and clarified to Clara's family, along with an explanation of ways in which to cope. After a brief period during which Clara had in-home care, she was institutionalized.

We use this example to make a point. At some stage it is highly likely we all will be faced with the matter of dealing with loved ones who need help. Many of us will be put in a position of providing care. Many more will be faced with difficult decisions regarding care.

Complications will arise as decisions are explored not alone, but with other family members. Ethical, moral, religious, financial, and emotional conflicts and decisions will confront us. How we, as individuals, deal with them and what decisions we make will impact significantly on the quality of life and in some cases on the length of life of our loved ones. It is a weighty responsibility, one with which most of us are ill equipped to deal. But one which virtually all of us will be forced to accept, in one way or another.

For many, it will be a difficult and traumatic shift in behavior. We will have to surrender a secondary role for a primary role. We will have to understand that there often comes a point in life where the child who has been nurtured, counseled, and cared for by the adult must reverse the roles and become the provider and nurturer to the ill or otherwise infirm adult.

How each of us responds to the options available to us will differ greatly.

Some will be able to provide for their parents while they remain in their own homes, making regular visits, sharing occasional meals, assisting them with shopping and getting to doctor's appointments, offering a sympathetic ear, making sure younger family members stop by to share some time with Grandma, Grandpop, or the older aunt or uncle.

Some of us will be able to care for our elderly ill or infirm loved ones by taking them into our own homes and providing a warm, comfortable setting, with food, medicine, and fulfilling special needs.

But in our uniquely and increasingly mobile society, where families often are separated by wide geographical distances, the prospect is that we will not be able to provide for our elderly in the ways mentioned above.

The greater likelihood is that what care is provided will be by others, not family, and it will be a combination of volunteers and professionals.

For many people now in their fifties and sixties, the memory of the nuclear family, with festive annual reunions, several generations within easy driving distance, aunts, uncles, and cousins with whom we regularly interact, has given way to the realization that our changing socio-economic environment has turned us into a nation of nomads.

The telephone company notes that one in four people are likely to change residences each year. Demographers advise us that it is not unusual for the average adult to change jobs four times during a lifetime and that those changes frequently require a geographical move. A growing military population means that many individuals and families move on an average of every two years.

People employed by corporations in management positions have long understood that moving is just part of the job. Stories abound of moves from coast to coast, city to city, with each promotion.

We are a nation on the move. Yet our elderly generally stay put or, if personal resources permit, sometimes move to warmer climates. Even then, with such a move, the elderly leave family and lifetime friends.

Fifty years ago, the blink of an eye in the evolution of our nation, families resided primarily in the same community and we took care of each other. Family doctors were just that. Single older women played a valuable role administering to the needs of other family members.

The literature of the first half of this century has carefully etched in many minds the semitragic figure of the spinster whose life was spent in a small semi-rural community, caring for parent or sibling, dreaming of a love that was lost or never existed, which would take her away from a life of servitude.

We have changed: as a nation, as families, as individuals. Even where families have stayed in the same community, the number of two-salary families has increased dramatically, meaning that there is no longer a family member available to look after older relatives when help is needed.

The neighborhood we valued as we grew up no longer seems as attractive as we begin to raise our own children. We seek larger yards, parks, better schools. We move away from the neighborhood we called home, to the suburbs, in search of that evasive "better life" so many of us have sought.

Out parents, remembering the Depression of the '30s and the sacrifices of World War II wanted a "better life" for their children. And with increasing frequency, that meant moving away from what had been core family.

That is not to say that the family structure of old no longer exists. It does. But it does so in significantly decreasing numbers. Because of this trend, care of our elderly has taken on new and significant dimensions.

Many decisions that used to be made in family conclaves, around a kitchen table, now are made by phone, by family members who may see each other—and older relatives—once or twice a year. Decisions that in the past may have evolved over several days of individual interaction are now frequently placed in the laps of family members who are closest to the scene. And closest, for many families, may still mean hundred of miles. Many of us, sometimes in welcome relief, sometimes with no little guilt, and sometimes with a feeling of frustration and helplessness, abdicate responsibility for the care of elderly loved ones to the practicality of "real life."

For many people, particularly those with families and responsibilities of their own, the cost in time and money of jetting halfway across the nation several times a year to spend time with a parent, aunt, uncle, or dear friend appears (and frequently is) substantial. There is, after all, the practical side of things to consider. Our own children have school, meetings, lessons, and sports. We have activities of our own, missing work is difficult, and it is *so hard.* . . .

It *is* hard! There is no denying that. But we must each understand what our responsibility is, what options we have, and what we can do about it. Throughout this book, we have tried to get across one important message: We must educate ourselves and plan ahead, because most of us will be confronted at some point with the need to make health-care and quality-of-life decisions about older loved ones, or about ourselves, in the event there are no younger loved ones to look after us.

HOW DO WE BEGIN?

The fact is that most of us do not plan ahead when it comes to dealing with the subject of health care. We probably put more effort into planning our vacations. No one wants to admit that Mom and Dad are getting older (or that *we* are getting older) and very likely will need help in living in the future.

Further it is hard to think of once strong, healthy, and active people as in need of a walker, requiring numerous medicines, falling frequently, losing eyesight and even memory.

Denial is a strong factor in our thinking. Most of us tend to put depressing thoughts out of our minds. And instead we will put off confronting difficult decisions until crisis precipitates action.

But we must learn to accept reality and deal with it. We and our loved ones will become elderly. We won't be able to maneuver as well in the future, we are likely to suffer debilitating illnesses, we may need help with living, and we very likely will have to surrender some control over our own lives.

As we learn to accept this reality, we also must learn to change our way of thinking. We must look at the reality with as positive an attitude as we can. Fortunately, there are options most of us will have. And there is good in virtually every option.

To surrender some control may mean that someone else now will take responsibility for tasks such as laundry or grocery shopping, which we may not have enjoyed anyway. As a result, we eliminate the continual frustration and stress associated with attempting to do those things we cannot. Having help getting in and out of the tub or shower can avoid a fall that could result in serious injury.

CALVIN

This is a story of cooperation between client, attorney, physician, and home-care agency.

We received a call from a physician who indicated he had a stroke patient ready for discharge, eager to go home, and able to do so with proper care. The care had to be twenty-four-hour, because he was still partially paralyzed on the right side.

Calvin, a former stockbroker, had once been an avid golfer. His home was on the edge of a golf course near the ocean. Slight in stature, he was not particularly distinguished in his appearance.

Calvin also had a history of chronic high blood pressure. We knew it was important to monitor his medicines. The physician had done an excellent job in this regard. But Calvin's prognosis was still not good. The physician did not anticipate he would live more than six months to a year.

Calvin is also fortunate in that he has a friend who lives next door with whom he has been friends for years, and who has Calvin's power of attorney.

His lawyer sees Calvin regularly and we evaluate him on a monthly basis and keep the bank and the attorney informed regularly. Unfortunately, at age eighty-eight, and after five years of our caregiving,

Calvin is running out of money.

He has lived well beyond the time anyone would have expected, but the quality of his life is excellent. His nurses take him out to art centers, to get ice cream, to shows, and for rides. They have become very close to Calvin and, in fact, have foregone increases in salary to continue to care for him.

Because Calvin insists on remaining at home, the attorney has decided that, if it is necessary, the home will be sold on the condition that Calvin may remain there as long as he lives. This will provide him with the needed extra income. Calvin is well cared for in every respect and he is happy.

The point here is that there are options that can be explored if people care enough to examine them.

How we attack problems related to our elderly, whether well or infirm, is vital to their—and often our—well-being. We can do what we do with so many of our children—put them in front of the TV set and let the tube provide elder care or we can work with friends and other relatives to find ways and means of involving these people and providing them with a reason for living. The choice, in large measure, is ours.

WHEN IN DOUBT, COMMUNICATE

Perhaps the biggest problem we confront as individuals involved with elderly loved ones, well or infirm, is a lack of communication. Although we may talk to these people regularly, too often we talk *at* people and not *with* them. Communication is, after all, a two-way street. One must convey a message to someone and that person must receive the message. Then the first person must listen to the second and make certain the message has been received as it was conveyed.

We do not suggest that the communication process—especially with older loved ones—is an easy one. To the contrary. But if we are to deal intelligently with matters relating to these people, we must work to open up lines of communication.

We must explain clearly the things affecting their lives. We must talk about the need for them to take medicines, to make certain their finances are in order, to alleviate misconceptions, to listen to their concerns, and let them know their options and your recommendations where appropriate.

Before a hospital stay, you can make sure that the doctor has provided all the information the patient needs to be reassured. You can obtain all the information that is necessary to make well-informed decisions about in-home care after the hospital stay, or nursing-home care if that is necessary.

It has been our experience that the more an individual knows about things that are unfamiliar or fearsome, the more comfortable the individual will be in confronting realities.

You, as a friend or family member, can do a great deal to relieve anxieties by putting yourself in the older person's place and asking yourself, "What would I like to know about my options?"

Another way to deal with the situation is to ask the older loved one what he or she would like to know about what is going on around them. Find out where they are uncomfortable or confused. In some cases, a parent or older friend may be too proud to ask for help and you may have to volunteer.

Finally, in some cases, you may have to step in and take charge. An individual may be in financial trouble. Bills may not be paid or checks written without balancing the checkbook, perhaps with chronic overdrafts, while Social Security checks sit on a table or in a pile of papers, undeposited. You may have to gently but firmly insist on assuming control of an individual's finances if he or she is no longer able to exercise prudent management of funds.

This is not an easy decision to make or put into effect. It is easier, however, if you and other family members discuss the circumstance in advance, if you agree as to how the situation will be handled should it arise, and if you and others, if possible, carefully explain the problems and the benefits of shifting responsibility to others.

Similarly, if you believe your parent, relative, or friend would benefit from in-home care to relieve him or her from tasks or chores no longer possible to handle without significant difficulty or the prospect of accidental injury, discuss the options well in advance, give the individual some time to think about it, and provide him or her with the positive aspects of such a decision.

FLORA

A strong-willed woman in a decidedly matriarchal Italian household who refused to speak English, Flora was a stroke victim who had recovered well in a convalescent hospital and insisted on returning home.

However, Flora was at a point where she was unable to adequately care for herself, but was unwilling to admit it and strongly resisted having help from a caregiver.

Five well-educated adult children were unable to take charge of their mother's life and demand that she obtain help. Thus, bills piled up and the power company shut off her electricity. The house was cold and dark.

While Flora really wanted to see her children and grandchildren, her pride prevented her from telling them. Further, the children, knowing her attitude and obstinance, didn't want their mother to live with them. So Flora's situation grew worse and the family interactions more tense.

We ultimately received a request to look into Flora's situation. We urged the family to get together and make a joint decision on what to do about their mother.

When no action was taken, and with the realization that something had to be done, we threatened to bring Adult Protective Services into the case. As a result, the family pulled together and made arrangements for their mother to spend several months with each child on a rotating basis, thus making the mother happy and relieving themselves of the guilt they were experiencing while the woman was living alone.

Many new ideas confronting older people are often hard to accept initially, but much easier to deal with once they are accepted. The important thing is to accept personal responsibility and take action when action is needed.

It is seldom that an older person will voluntarily

acknowledge that they are no longer able to make good decisions on their own and ask you to take over certain responsibilities. It is far more likely that you will have to do so on your own.

TIMING IS IMPORTANT

Is there ever a "good" time to approach difficult subjects such as relinquishing certain controls over your life? We believe there is. It is while the individual is still able to think clearly and understand what needs to be done. This also allows the individual to maintain control over who handles his or her affairs.

Keep in mind that the individual, even in the most positive of circumstances, may not make the decision you would make, but it is his or her life. They have the right to make the decision. (However, be wary of letting situations get out of hand. Remember the story of Dutch in Chapter 4.)

You nevertheless can initiate discussions on what happens in the event of life-threatening illness. Should heroic means be used to prolong life? When should someone take over the financial matters? Who should be appointed as the person with "power of attorney"? Has the individual provided "durable power of attorney for health care," which is a different situation than simple power of attorney? Investigate conservatorship.

You may wish to initiate discussion on where a will is kept, who prepared it and when, and whether it needs to be updated. What is the individual's situation regarding insurance and other important papers? Do they have any financial obligations? With their finances in perspective, what care options are open to them?

If you are unprepared to bring the issues to a direct discussion, we recommend clipping articles on the subjects and dropping them in the mail or at the individual's home to get them thinking. More often than not, it will come back to you at a later date, frequently in the form of a suggestion from the individual, as if it were his or her original idea. You have planted the seed.

The important thing is to generate discussion and bring the subject out on the table. Dealing with it after the fact usually creates more problems. Letting a problem go unattended never solved or improved it.

TEDDY

Not all our client/patients are elderly. Some of the most touching and trying are young people. Teddy was such a person. He was nine when we met him, a hemophiliac who had contracted AIDS as a result of a blood transfusion.

We cared for Teddy for almost a year. During this time, because AIDS has no cure, he gradually became worse, dropping to a skeletal thirty-four pounds at the time he died. Also during this time, the family's financial resources dwindled to nothing. Their insurance coverage ran out and they had to rely upon available community services.

Several agencies had turned Teddy down, apparently because of his AIDS status, at the point where he began to require in-home care. We provided care for him until close to the end.

His situation was heartrending, not only because of his age and the effects of the disease, but because the community-at-large rejected him. Parents of other students protested when Teddy's parents attempted to enroll him in school in the fall. Ultimately, trustees of the school district decided he would be better served by having private tutors at home.

Two of Teddy's brothers are also hemophiliacs and, like him, require periodic blood transfusions. Teddy was an inspiration to them, to his parents, and to us. He never complained and remained cheerful, always looking at the bright side of things. His parents, instead of being angry at the community that had rejected Teddy at the time when he needed acceptance most, felt that the community had missed an opportunity.

With Teddy as an example, his father observed, lessons about living in pain—and preparing to die— "could have been shared beyond his small circle of family, church, and friends. Children could (have gained) empathy, understanding, and kindness. Lessons would have been taught there which would be invaluable to children for the rest of their lives."

We use this story to introduce Chapter Six because it involves a full range of emotions—love, fear, happiness, anger, kindness, and more. Feelings and emotions are key elements in every caring situation we encounter.

6. Feelings

DOTTIE

For most of her life, Dottie was an active business-woman, a take-charge sort of person. Today, in her mid-eighties, she is arthritic, with constant pain that makes walking difficult. A tiny four feet, eight inches tall, Dottie nevertheless is used to being in charge of almost any situation. Opinionated, biased, talkative, and self-sufficient, Dottie always was meticulously dressed, complete with hat and gloves. Her quaint cottage home is filled with tapestry foot stools, intricate needlecraft, and family heirlooms. Her love of animals and travel are evident.

Dottie's husband, a delightful man with cap, cane, and walking shorts, is also ill, and Dottie is angry. She is upset because after many years of taking care of her husband, of being the principle wage earner, she feels now is his time to care for her, and he isn't able. So, Dottie, as a means of displaying her anger and frustration, has been making life difficult for herself and her husband. She refuses a wheelchair, won't wear her teeth at times, and feeds her food to the birds.

The couple has two daughters residing in distant cities. They realize that something has to be done to relieve the situation and to provide for both parents. But when the time came to make a decision, they were unable to act.

Recently the daughters visited our office. They also visited several other local agencies and convalescent homes. They had made several previous visits, each time asking detailed questions. Most recently, when asked why they had not yet made a decision, they responded, "We just can't do that to our parents. We just can't take away their independence."

CHARLENE

Charlene, aged sixty-five, is a former high-school gym teacher. She is tall, slender, in good physical condition, and looks younger than her age. She resides in a residential care home. Charlene is clinically depressed, believing that she has no reason to continue living. At the time we were consulted, she had not had a bath in a month.

Once outgoing and vivacious, she was now quiet and subdued. Her tiny, spartan room displayed an interest in historical novels and sports magazines.

When her daughter came to visit, Charlene took a bath, put on clean clothes, and looked presentable. As soon as the daughter left, she would put the clean clothes away, put on the dirty ones, and go back to her old routine.

Her daughter is a rigid, distant, prideful woman who, though repulsed by her mother's depressed condition, resisted for months doing anything about the situation. She, too, was unable to act.

Appearances are deceiving. The people at the residential care home were concerned that she didn't bathe or comb her hair or, in many instances, get out of bed on a day-to-day basis.

The operators of the facility, noting this behavior, called us. Charlene would have nothing to do with us. We called the daughter and explained the mother's situation. The daughter, in turn, denied our claims, suggesting that the residential care facility was just looking for ways to have others do their job.

We pointed out that the mother was a clinically depressed person who needed a nurse-patient relationship, which our caregiver could provide. The daughter replied that she simply needed a companion who could come in for two hours on a Friday afternoon and see that her mother had a bath and was dressed.

We also pointed out that what Charlene needed was to get up, bathe, and get dressed several times a week, to take her medicine, take a walk, get some ice cream, and get out of the building. The daughter refused to listen. We do not know what ultimately happened to Charlene, but we know that without help, she very likely would continue deteriorating and end up in a mental institution.

The tragedy is that Charlene could have been helped. It was a classic case of denial. Both Charlene and Dottie are victims of neglect—in this case, by their own, well-meaning children.

The February 22, 1990, edition of the Monterey *Herald*, in an article on Legal Services for Seniors noted the executive director reported that in January, 1990, he had nine cases of adult abuse, and "in 90 percent of the cases, the child of the client is the abuser."

EMOTIONS

In both cases, the daughters felt they were doing what they could, but both were letting emotional feelings get in the way of actions that might relieve substantial pressures on themselves and on their parents.

In both instances, the use of a qualified, in-home care service at an earlier date could have made a significant difference.

Charlene, with regular visits by someone who demonstrated an interest, monitored antidepressant medication, and provided companionship, could once again become a valuable member of society.

Dottie, with someone to prepare meals for herself and her husband, to administer their medicines, and to take them outside from time to time, would likely refocus her thoughts more positively.

People who are older and ill are frequently frightened. They rarely admit their fright and, as a result, they can become angry, manipulative, and verbally abusive. What they really want is assurance that someone really cares about them; that they aren't alone and unwanted.

Children, on the other hand, worry and experience great anxiety in dealing with the problems of their parents.

Both sets of feelings are real and should not be ignored. The questions of how to handle feelings and what to do about the situations with which we are confronted are worth exploring. We believe a cardinal rule for those concerned about older loved ones is to confront the situation directly.

First, realize that you are not the only ones confronted with these problems. Second, understand that frequently we can obtain help from professionals who deal with these situations daily. Third, and most important from our experience, a difficult situation, left unresolved, only becomes more difficult.

Frequently, older people know something must be done about their situation, but for various reasons don't or won't do anything about it themselves. They worry about the unknown, what will happen to them. They need to have the subject discussed in as positive a way as possible, lovingly, yet firmly.

PERSONAL RIGHTS

Both you and the older parent or other loved one have rights. Those rights must be discussed, understood, and respected.

They have the right to expect they will be treated fairly, with dignity, and in a caring manner. They also have the right to expect they will not be abused, allowed to live in a degrading state, or have their basic needs ignored.

You, the son or daughter, relative, or friend, have rights as well. You have the right not to be verbally, emotionally, or physically abused. You must be treated fairly. Your needs must be recognized and respected.

In short, in dealing with the needs of a loved one, both parties must be treated with care and concern.

Both must accept, as well, that the needs of the other will very likely have to be compromised somewhat as a result of the change in lifestyle required to solve the older person's problems.

Understanding of those facts is the first step toward solving the problem of how to care for an older loved one in need.

MARTHA

Martha is a proud, tiny eighty-year-old, whose still-brunette hair is wild and wiry. She lives in a wonderful, old stone house, amid stuffed birds and old furnishings. In the front yard is an old stagecoach wagon wheel.

Martha is connected to oxygen by tubing that she must carry with her wherever she goes. Once a heavy smoker, she now suffers from the ravages of emphysema.

She needs help. At the very least, she needs someone to assist her with the cleaning in a way that does not stir up the pollen and dust that aggravate her condition.

But Martha is stubborn. She is reluctant to give up control of her life, to have a stranger in the house, and to admit she isn't as self-sufficient as she used to be.

This is complicated by another common situation. Her children are intimidated and are reluctant to intervene. Martha has the resources to have in-home care that could prolong her life and certainly make it easier. But her family is worried that by intervening they might bring about alienation and, with it, possible disinheritance. Nothing is done.

MAGGIE

Maggie, a stout, determined woman in her sixties, of central-European origin, had lived alone for a number of years, having lost her husband to cancer. She had come to be comfortable with the freedom her independence afforded her. It enabled her to do things she didn't feel she could do while her husband was alive.

Now she has diabetes and problems with her legs that restrict her mobility. Her eyes are failing and she requires daily dosages of insulin.

Maggie was not quite prepared for the idea of having in-home care and didn't immediately like the idea.

But now, after several months of visits, she looks forward to seeing someone who cares, with whom she can talk and who visits her daily to assist with specific needs. She is living a different life, but she realizes that with help it is a significant improvement over the alternative.

"WHAT CAN I DO?"

A parent has been hospitalized and is about to be released. A mother develops a mental impairment. An uncle has a fall. A father, living alone, begins to deteriorate because of poor diet and inactivity.

Although they shouldn't be, these circumstances are often unexpected. In some instances, months or even years pass between visits by family members and changes are pronounced. "Dad seems to be slipping" or "I'm worried about the way the house is looking. Mom was such a meticulous housekeeper" are phrases heard frequently in our office.

These are signs that someone may soon need help. They may not be as evident as emphysema or a broken hip, but they are signals worth noting.

BEGIN EXPLORING OPTIONS

The signals suggest that parent and child should begin considering options. The first tentative explorations between the two or among all family members should begin.

Tough questions need to be asked, such as "If you were to need help in your daily routine, how would you want to handle it?" Or "What would you do if your driver's license were revoked or you suddenly became ill and couldn't get out and around?"

Also at this time, some discussion is in order regarding what care options are available.

ROLE REVERSALS

Often at times like this, a role reversal begins to take place. The parent becomes the child and the child the parent. We have seen it happen countless times. We have heard it in the way a middle-aged child talks to an elderly parent.

This family role reversal frequently takes place with great difficulty. The parent—or older loved one, if not a parent—struggles with the idea, let alone the process. He or she resents the surrendering of control, resists the loss of independence, and has difficulty accepting that a real need exists.

At the same time, there are situations where an older person gladly surrenders the decision-making process. He or she is relieved to have someone arrange for their well-being. Many older people realize that they are having trouble making decisions or that it is a worrisome process to them and they welcome someone else doing something for them at this stage in their lives. It is not always easy to predict how an older person will react when confronted with decisions related to their care.

BEHAVIOR AND ANXIETY

Choices at this stage are often difficult and always heartrending. Restricting someone else's independence, reacting to them on a different level, with roles reversed, making decisions for them when—for a great deal of your life—they made decisions for you, are not tasks most of us will adapt to easily.

Part of the reason many of us fail to respond to the needs of loved ones is learned behavior and anxiety.

Learned behavior refers to the fact that the parent or elderly loved one generally has been an authority figure most of our lives. We have learned to behave in a certain way toward that person. It is uncomfortable changing our image of the individual and reversing the roles.

We have to undo traditional images and roles. We often do not want to accept that a parent no longer can adequately care for him or herself. We recoil at the reality of knowing that we no longer have the security of knowing our parents are always there for us, to care for us in time of need.

Because of this, anxiety develops. Anxiety often manifests itself in a form of mild depression and an inability to act decisively. We question over and over whether we are doing the right thing and whether we did all we could in the past. We begin to feel shame at our inability to care for the individual ourselves and guilt about the fact that we may not have paid as much attention to our parents as we should have.

But younger members of a family must overcome guilt and anxiety and act when older people no longer recognize their own inability to care for themselves. Someone must make decisions when older people are reluctant to give up control over their own lives, but are no longer able to maintain control.

How do we deal with situations like this? How can we handle anxiety, frustration, anger, revulsion, rejection, and guilt?

The first and most important consideration is the person's well-being. If you keep in mind the clear question of whether you are acting in the best interests of the individual, you will overcome some of the emotional blocks you are experiencing. Ask yourself, "Am I acting in this person's best interest?" If you sincerely believe your decision meets this test, your anxiety level will be substantially reduced.

Next we must accept the fact that the feelings are real, then get them out in the open. Discuss them. You may find or establish a support group of people like yourself who are experiencing the same feelings for the same reasons. In any case, talk with friends and relatives about how you feel.

Then, learn to separate emotions from facts, feelings from realities, the important from the unimportant reasons for feeling the way you do. Your feelings may have been delaying your decisions. But exploring options in a rational, unemotional manner will help alleviate some of the anxiety. Finally, accept the fact it is normal to have such feelings. Virtually everyone has them and most people find a way to deal with them. You will, too.

If you have been able to communicate with a loved one as an adult and the relationship is a good one, the level of trust created between you is likely to make changes easier. You will find it easier to communicate the reasons behind your decisions and the other person will be in a more receptive frame of mind.

It helps to understand that if you have a strained relationship over a long period, it is likely to be a more difficult transition than if you and the person were on very good terms.

As in-home care administrators, we see situations like this regularly. It is simply unrealistic to expect a poor relationship to improve substantially, especially in times of stress.

PROMISES, PROMISES

Often we hear older people plead with their children or spouse, "Don't ever put me away in a nursing home," Or "Promise me you'll stay with me and personally take care of me." These are understandable requests.

We urge people not to make these kinds of promises. Rather, we suggest they promise only that they will do what is in the best interest of the person at the time, and leave it at that.

Avoid making promises under stress without the facts and some perspective on the situation. This also will help reduce anxiety later on.

At times, the only answer is a nursing or convalescent home. But often loved ones can remain at home, comfortable in familiar surroundings, with assistance from in-home care providers. This should be a welcome option for most people faced with decisions on how their loved ones are to be cared for.

Generally speaking, with proper care, most elderly people can avoid having to go to a nursing or convalescent home, except under the most critical of circumstances.

LAURA

A devout Christian Scientist, Laura had managed to go through life without encountering life-threatening illnesses, refusing medical care for more routine matters, while keeping her faith intact.

When we met her she had developed a lesion on her face that was starting to press into her optic and maxillary nerves, causing loss of vision and difficulty in chewing. She had spent almost a year in a Christian Science home in the San Francisco area where Vaseline and gauze had been applied to the lesion while she applied Christian Science principles.

A very proper, yet generally progressive woman, Laura had been an executive secretary in the Los Angeles film community during her working life. Through good advice from her employer, she had saved and invested wisely and, as a result, was not wanting for funds.

Laura had a niece and nephew to whom she had provided power of attorney. As her problem grew more pronounced, the niece and nephew pleaded with Laura to have medical attention. She refused. They persisted and eventually she had minor facial surgery but not the radical suggested by the doctor.

Laura was no more accepting of our nursing care. There was no way she would allow us to tend to her lesion. When we took her to the doctor, she would lie about her follow up care. In fact, she was demanding of the nurses that they sit by her bed, hold her hand, and respond to her every whim. At the same time, she rejected the medical care they were there to provide. She would not allow the caregivers to cook in her kitchen, forbade them to sit on her couch, and, in general, made life miserable for them. We had great difficulty keeping nurses on the job. Finally Laura, denying further medical help was needed, despite the fact that her facial lesion had proved cancerous, moved back to the Christian Scientist home in San Francisco Bay area. We had no follow up information, but the prognosis was not good.

7. In All Directions

"I don't ever want to go to a nursing home. They're just warehouses of people waiting to die."

This position, advanced by a California resident, is not unusual. Repeated stories of abuses and lack of care in nursing or convalescent homes have made many people wary of the prospect of becoming a patient in one. Martin is one of those people.

MARTIN

At age seventy-three, Martin takes pride in his appearance and in his independence. He is an avid walker. Recently, he has reluctantly begun to use a cane and his arthritis has become a frustration. But Martin is looking forward to spring training games of the Major League Baseball teams and follows local, national, and world affairs with interest. Several times a years he jets off to various parts of the country to visit his children and their families. His attitude is positive, except where it concerns nursing homes.

What options does Martin have if he becomes so ill that he can no longer remain alone in his own home in this small California town?

The answer? Not many. But because he is financially independent, Martin has more options than most.

First, he can move to a retirement community. Second, he might consider a residential care facility if his health begins to create problems dealing with life's more normal situations. Third, he can hire a full-time caregiver at home. Fourth, he can move in with one of his children, assuming one can and will accommodate him. And finally, despite his concerns, he could move to a nursing or convalescent-care facility.

Let's examine these options.

RETIREMENT COMMUNITIES

There are various types of retirement communities. Most are expensive. Some are very exclusive, built around golf courses, tennis courts, and in resort areas in warm climates.

Most retirement communities do not have facilities to provide for the health care of patients. Some do. In most cases, these are little more than simple infirmaries for short-term problems.

On the other hand, there are a few retirement communities, which, for a hefty fee, offer to care for a person, whatever the situation, until he or she dies.

For many reasonably well-to-do people, the thought of a retirement community where time can be spent in leisurely activity, among others of a compatible age—a reward for having worked hard over most of a lifetime—is hugely appealing. But for many, the realities are not always positive.

JENNIE

A perky, lively little woman, Jennie resided in a retirement community outside Carmel, California, in a scenic hillside setting. She thrived on the interaction she had with friends and enjoyed the many benefits the community provided in terms of group activities and field trips. She looked forward to spending the rest of her life in this setting.

Jennie's family resided in San Francisco and she, an independent type, fended quite well for herself.

However, Jennie fell and broke her hip, a situation not uncommon among older women. When she was released from the hospital, Jennie realized she couldn't return to her retirement community because she would need nursing care for some weeks. Her choice? A residential care home. Here Jennie could benefit from twenty-four-hour care, someone to fix her meals, and the company of others.

At this convenient location, in sharp contrast to her sloping hillside home, she had a steady stream of visitors her own age. Jennie thrived.

At about this stage, Jennie got involved with an attorney with a number of elderly clients. The attorney, looking into Jennie's financial situation, reasoned she should go back to her home and obtain a live-in companion. The cost would be less than at the residential care home, he reasoned. Despite the reservations of Jennie and her relatives, the attorney prevailed.

The result? Jennie soon felt isolated from friends who found it more difficult to visit her home because of the steeply sloping driveways and walkways. Jennie's untrained live-in help proved unsatisfactory. Left unattended at one point, Jennie fell and again broke her hip. She went back to the hospital. This situation repeated itself twice within a year. Jennie became mentally and physically more dependent and ended up in a nursing home.

Jennie once confided to us that she was happiest and felt most comfortable in the residential care facility. The key to this case was the fact that the doctor, adhering to the attorney's wishes that she stay at home, failed to prescribe the level of in-home care and, as a result, the attorney obtained the cheapest rather than the best qualified care. And, it was not the role of the retirement community to care for Jennie's health and welfare.

While we are advocates of in-home care we recognize, and so should our readers, that this form of health care is not always the most desirable in every case. And, in Jennie's case, once she reached a certain stage in her health, going back to a home in a retirement community to live alone or with unqualified help was also not the best solution.

A point worth considering is a fact that most people, when they think of a retirement community, do not think about what will happen if, for health reasons, they no longer can stay in their new quarters. Frequently they find themselves paying the monthly retirement home fees and additional costs for residential or nursing home care.

RESIDENTIAL CARE HOMES

Our position has been and remains that people are most comfortable and happiest in surroundings that are as close to a home setting as possible. If they can't remain in their own home, they can find a homelike setting in a residential care facility.

Most residential care facilities are limited to a small number of residents, usually less than ten.

Here the individual is most likely to find a private room in which they can have personal items, including paintings, photographs, and furniture.

Meals are prepared with the resident's specific needs and preferences in mind. They are served in the company of other residents so there is some interaction with others.

People in a residential care facility do not require skilled nursing care. The reasons they are there vary but would range from someone whose mental and/or physical condition has been impaired to someone who simply is elderly and unable to fend for him or herself.

People who reside in residential care facilities generally have not wanted to move out of their homes, but had an impairment significant enough to warrant their needing monitoring twenty-four hours a day. Since the cost of twenty-four-hour private duty care may be prohibitive for some, this type of facility offers another option.

PROBLEM AREAS

Residential care homes are not a panacea and, like any other form of health care, need to be carefully assessed both before and during the period an individual is a resident.

The term *residential care facility* is indigenous to

California. In Illinois they are referred to as community living facilities, and in Florida, they are known as adult congregate living facilities.

You should know ahead of time that most such facilities operate on a tight budget; they must run cost-effectively. They are not large enough to be able to make a profit from quantity. One vacant bed in a six-bed facility, for instance, means that one-sixth of the home's income is gone. Yet mortgages and personnel costs continue.

Residential care facilities usually have some social schedule, but this is not and should not be their primary focus. The staff is there to assist residents with problems they may have, such as monitoring what medicine to take and when, getting to and from doctor appointments, helping dress or undress, and getting in and out of the bathtub.

Staffing for such facilities runs from trained nurses' assistants and even, on occasion, a licensed vocational or practical nurse, to "sitters" or "housekeepers" with no nursing training or skills.

In most states, there is no requirement that residential care homes have employees with any skills. And this is where problems begin to arise.

In situations where no nursing training is required, residential care homes are likely to provide only the services required. This means a place to sleep, three meals a day, and general supervision. While they may be doing what they are supposed to do, the level of care is questionable.

Those facilities that are licensed are generally under the jurisdiction of the social services, not the health department. The concerns of the social services department generally are that there is adequate fire protection, it is clean, and there are ramps for wheelchairs. However, licensing requirements vary widely by state and some states do not require a license to operate at all.

While these obviously are important factors, even more important, we feel, is patient care.

LORAINE

An accomplished interior designer and business-woman, Loraine was, in her prime, a tall, strong, hearty, outgoing woman, meticulous in her appearance and detailed in her approach to business.

At age seventy-five, Loraine began to slow down. She required a hip replacement, which was stunningly successful. She recovered quickly and continued her interest in sports and gardening, generating great pleasure from the beauty of her home.

Not long after, Loraine required a cataract operation. At the time, she was living in a retirement community that had an infirmary. About this time, we were contracted to provide occasional in-home care. Loraine had become unsteady as a result of several slight strokes that caused some dizziness, and she was beginning to feel the effects of osteoporosis.

Loraine was concerned with her deterioration, but was reluctant to share that concern with her family. The family, on the other hand, was alert to symptoms that their mother's health was deteriorating. She allowed piles of magazines to build up unread, changed her dietary habits to cover up for the fact that she could no longer lift the pots and pans, and dressed in an unusual manner.

Loraine's family subsequently moved her to a residential care home. In three months she was dead. While it is impossible to state unequivocally that the move caused her death, we are aware that she received only marginal care there, that people generally are happier in their own homes, and that she could have afforded in-home care of a better quality than she received at that residential care home.

WHAT TO LOOK FOR

What then should a family look for when choosing a residential care facility? First, we recommend that the family visit the facility both by appointment and unannounced. When you are expected, the facility will be prepared to display its best front. But it is when you are not expected, especially at mealtime, that you get a true picture of the place.

Talk to the residents. Find out how long they have been there and if they know the names of and are comfortable with the staff. Have they gotten to know the other residents? Are they all dressed during the day? Are the men clean-shaven and do the women have their hair cared for?

How are meals prepared? What is the quality of the food? Is the meal room or table attractive and pleasant?

Are the kitchen and bathroom(s) clean? How does the place smell? Is the yard well tended? Are staff members allowed to entertain visitors who would detract the attention of staff to residents?

Learn the requirements for entrance into the home and learn how one can be taken out of the home as well. Visits to the family member or friend should include assessment of their cleanliness and neatness, general comfort, eating habits, and personal grooming.

While it is important to look at licensing and even membership in a state or county association of residential care providers, these factors do not assure a level of care delivery. There exists all across the nation a need for stricter regulations on care delivery in residential care homes.

NURSING/CONVALESCENT HOMES

When should one consider a nursing or convalescent home? There are two times when a convalescent or nursing care facility seems appropriate. The first is when a patient's doctor prescribes that no other type of care is adequate.

The rationale for the doctor's prescribing such care is that the patient needs skilled nursing help, not generally available in the home or at a residential care facility. Frequently the patient requires specialized care and monitoring at a level that does not require hospitalization as we normally think of it, but does require twenty-four-hour or periodic highly skilled nursing care by a registered nurse.

Nursing homes should therefore be filled with people who cannot care for themselves. They provide care for people in long-term comas. They provide for people with Alzheimer's disease who have no family care providers.

It is not a happy atmosphere and, because most residents of nursing homes eventually die there, it is no wonder that people like Martin reject nursing/convalescent homes.

This is not to say that all nursing/convalescent homes are bad or that they don't serve a purpose. Many, probably most, provide care well and with concern for the patient. But like any institution, they deal with rules, routines, and regulators. They constantly fight the problem of hiring and maintaining quality staff, and the staff they do have is generally grossly underpaid. The national shortage of nurses hits all areas of patient care across the country. Entry to and exit from a nursing/convalescent home means filling our countless papers and exasperating formalities.

Patients frequently must wait for attention. Many feel disoriented and alone in an unfamiliar surrounding with strange people, a routine dictated by someone else, lack of responsiveness by staff and often being treated like a child.

Often when a patient enters a convalescent hospital or nursing home, the assumption is that now everything will be taken care of—monetary, legal, and health needs. Not so!

Just as an attorney frequently does not concern him or herself with a client's health-care needs and an accountant doesn't concern him or herself with a client's legal problems, the convalescent hospital usually doesn't handle all three. When they do, the quality of the service is often poor.

In one convalescent hospital with which we have had experience, a former director of nursing has taken over significant control of patient's finances and the issue of additional care, supplementing care provided by the hospital.

In most situations, the people fulfilling this role are not experienced enough to be able to dictate how expenditures should be made in the best interest of the patients.

We were called in by a bank trust officer to take a look at charges being made by the convalescent hospital that the bank was questioning. Checks were being cashed for clients about which the trustee had no knowledge.

When the bank inquired directly, hospital authorities simply stated it was their policy to allow private-duty nurses to access the checkbooks of their patients.

The director of nursing was hiring private-duty nurses to care for some patients if she felt she didn't have enough staff to handle the case load. The cost of these nurses was being charged back to the patient, without prior approval of anyone.

Since most of these people were wealthy and had bank trust accounts, she seldom got any flack from family or bank personnel until the trust officer who contacted us discovered a great deal of money was going out on top of the amount paid to the hospital.

We discovered that private-duty nurses—often untrained aides—had access to people's checkbooks and cash, and were provided salaries way above the standard for even skilled nurses.

We reported back that the costs were exorbitant, people were not being monitored, and, in one case, a person who was supposed to have a private-duty nurse was not being cared for because the private-duty nurse was helping the director of nursing with other patients. This appeared to be a fairly regular occurrence.

The trust department then wanted us to take over their client's cases. The director of nursing firmly rejected our recommendations and told the trust department she would make sure the patients were discharged if they persisted.

The trust department then backed off. Both the conservators and the patients were intimidated by the hospital official. Leaving would have been too traumatic.

The convalescent hospital has since been cited several times by state authorities for this and other abuses, but it is still operating as of this writing.

It is costly to be a patient in a nursing/convalescent home. Less so perhaps than in an acute-care hospital, but also more financially stressful because nursing/convalescent care is only partially covered by Medicare and Medicaid. At present, nursing homes also serve people who require long-term nursing care but for whom acute care hospitalization would be neither economically feasible nor possible from the hospital's standpoint.

DELBERT

Delbert is a small, meticulously dressed man, retired after many years as a custodian for a high school. He and his wife were married fifty-two years when she had a stroke. The couple had no children. Delbert was devastated. He loved his wife very much and wanted only the best for her.

Her physician suggested to Delbert that his wife go to a convalescent hospital. Not aware of the other options available to them, Delbert acquiesced.

114

Shortly thereafter, Delbert came to visit his wife and was stunned and angered to find her in a bed soaked with urine, unattended. The wife, partially paralyzed and incontinent, could not care for herself. Delbert summoned a floor nurse and insisted that his wife be cleaned and the bedding changed.

The next day, he entered his wife's room to find her with her head stuck between the restraining bars of the bed, unable to free herself, Furious, Delbert confronted the nurse who, after extracting Delbert's wife from between the bars, informed him that she was the only person attending to twenty people and that she had no backup. She couldn't possibly monitor every patient at every moment.

Delbert removed his wife from the convalescent hospital after a neighbor suggested he bring his wife home. Upon consulting with his doctor, the doctor agreed with the choice. Unfortunately, the doctor originally gave Delbert no initial choice. Had he done so, the wife might have been spared the trauma of her experience.

RANDOLPH

A tall, angular man of ninety-two, Randolph was senile. A patient in a private room in a convalescent hospital, he frequently would get up at night and wander around his room. As a result, the hospital staff kept his room and windows locked.

However, one night Randolph, stark naked, began to wander and found the door to the adjoining room unlocked. He entered the room where he encountered a newly awakened, yet thoroughly alert elderly woman who, upon seeing this huge, naked man, screamed for help.

Frightened and bewildered, Randolph turned and ran through a window in the woman's room, falling three stories, and smashing the bones in his face upon impact.

Randolph subsequently died of the injuries and trauma. Had he been more closely monitored and had someone checked the doors and windows of his room that evening, a tragic event might not have occurred.

Nursing homes often average no more than one registered nurse for each seventeen patients and have only one aide for each floor on a normal shift. You have the right to inquire what the caregiver to patient ratio is at any time.

Further, just because there are nurses and aides on duty does not mean you or the patient will receive unlimited care. The average time a patient may see a registered nurse in an eight-hour shift is fifteen minutes. The average time for an aide is no more than thirty minutes.

Thinking that one needs twenty-four-hour care to prepare for emergencies may be faulty. These days, even small towns have a variety of technological appliances and devices that permit someone in trouble to notify a hospital or a rescue unit. These devices are attached to telephones and sometimes worn as bracelets, necklaces, or pins. Such devices enable individuals who previously felt they needed to be in a hospital setting to live well and with confidence at home.

Just because someone is admitted to a convalescent hospital is no assurance that they will be properly cared for.

IN-HOME HEALTH CARE

Another option is in-home care. This approach is particularly beneficial to a patient whose mental faculties are sound and who has either a potential for recovery or who has a period of time before an illness such as cancer becomes so bad they must be hospitalized or placed in a hospice. But most importantly, this could be the best option for those who suffer chronic long-term problems requiring nothing more than daily living assistance.

With this option, the patient has the benefits of familiar surroundings, the comfort of personal belongings, the freedom to eat what and when he or she wants, and the psychological plus of feeling at least partially in control.

Friends and family are more comfortable visiting a person who is ill at home rather than in the often depressing atmosphere of a nursing/convalescent facility.

While costs of a companion and nurses is not covered under Medicare or most insurance, except under certain and infrequent circumstances, neither are most costs of long-term nursing home care.

LIVING WITH CHILDREN

While living with children when you can no longer live alone often seems desirable, the decision should be approached carefully.

Too often well-meaning children say, "Of course Dad will come to live with us. What kind of children would we be if we turned him away?" With this statement, the children are expressing guilt. Their concern is not only for Dad, it is for how they feel and how others may perceive the situation.

It is possible, of course, that the circumstances might be ideal for Dad to live with an offspring. However, our experience suggests this is seldom the case.

No matter how much an older family member is loved, having that person around as a new member of an existing family creates additional burdens, both physical and psychological, which create stress in a household.

Children have to be more considerate of noise that would bother the older patient. The patient is cognizant of the fact that members of the family are being inconvenienced and their normal life interrupted because of his or her presence.

The older person will often have a tendency to try to stay out of the family's way, thus isolating him or herself. The family, on the other hand, often regards this as Dad or Mom's way of saying they would like to be by themselves.

Older people often have trouble accepting the fact that the son and daughter or niece and nephew are doing things differently than they would do them. Tempers become short when the hosts are confronted with suggestions on how things should be handled around the house.

Requests become demands. Suggestions become requests. Idle comments become dictums. Observations become criticisms. In short, tensions frequently arise and the whole family becomes uncomfortable and unhappy, often feeling trapped and not knowing how to get out of the situation.

On occasion, families are both willing and able to

, friendly man, Alva was employed for almost
years as a yard man—a combination gar-
leanup person, and Mr. Fixit—for the local
He loved the interaction with young people
job afforded him. At age sixty-five, Alva had
from his college job. For almost ten years he
within the community at various similar jobs.

Ruth, a cook in a local restaurant, enjoyed
with Alva in the yard and their garden in the
tates community in which they lived, was
ng the townspeople looked forward to seeing
e winter snow and winds subsided. At age
five, Alva's health began to decline. Within a
f seven weeks, he had to endure two car-
lar surgeries. His recovery was slow, his ac-
imited and his ability to earn a living disap-

t a year ago Alva, now eighty-three, had
cardiovascular operation. This time, while on
ating table, he suffered a severe stroke. Then
eks later, he underwent kidney surgery. The
these surgeries and the hospitalization was
s.

is stage in his life, Alva was forced to rely on
dollars per month Social Security payment

provide care for a loved one. A part of the house is set
aside for Dad or Mom and some privacy is accorded
while, at the same time, the individual can elect to be
part of the larger family if he or she chooses. Both
generations learn to live together again and one
sometimes complements the other.

This is, of course, harder to accomplish with the
plethora of two-income families. Often having someone to come in and help Mom and Dad a few times a
week lessens the strain and offers a needed respite
for the family as well as a change of pace for the older
adult.

In some situations, a well-meaning son or
daughter wishes Dad or Mom would come to live with
them in a distant city, not realizing that the parent
would have to leave friends and familiar surroundings and the independence he or she has treasured,
to become part of someone else's household. The
subject of living arrangements in times of illness
should be carefully discussed with the individuals in
question rather than assuming anything.

Regardless of the living situation, we cannot
repeat often enough the need to plan ahead. While
you or a loved one are *not* in need, find out what the
options are in your local setting. Visit the various
kinds of living arrangements. Talk with relatives who
might be willing to take in a family member, if that
option exists. Look at the costs involved and determine who accepts what responsibility.

ELEANOR

Probably one of our most eccentric patients,

Eleanor was one of our most colorful as well. We never knew how old she was because she would never tell us. She also had never obtained a Social Security number. And she was *never* referred to by her first name. We discovered that she was an heiress to a huge publishing fortune.

We were first called by her husband's personal secretary. Eleanor originally had an infected little toenail. She chose to ignore the initial problem and by the time she saw a doctor, the toe was infected to the point where she was advised to have it removed.

Vanity won out. Eleanor refused. She would not have her body mutilated, she said. The doctor warned her if the toe got worse, she would likely have to have her foot amputated. Still she refused. The infection got worse. Despite pleas from the doctor, she stubbornly rejected all advice.

When we were summoned, we were told we would have just five minutes with Eleanor. We were totally unprepared for what we found. The house was enormous, as was Eleanor's suite. The view from her bed provided a panorama of the Pacific Ocean rocks and seashore. Propped up in bed, completely made up, hair styled, Eleanor was in her finest boudoir. A naturally beautiful woman, and enormously aware of the fact, Eleanor's incredible vanity extended to the degree that she kept a large mirror in her bed so she could periodically look at herself.

We were introduced quite formally and told we could sit in a particular spot. The secretary rushed to provide a chair. At this point, Eleanor had lost her leg just below the knee. Her family had threatened to obtain a court order to require that she have treatment in a life-threatening situation and she finally gave in.

As a result of the loss o[...] off her life to friends, family [...] sary contacts. Her husband [...] wing of the house. She had [...] quarters once a week and o[...] sued a formal invitation.

After several months of n[...] a phone call from one of t[...] Eleanor appeared to be ha[...] One nurse called the doctor a[...] tor stated Eleanor died of p[...] heart. We believe this resul[...] from the emotional stress of [...] isolation.

8. C[...]

ALVA[...]

A gent[...]
twenty[...]
dener,[...]
college[...]
that h[...]
to reti[...]
worke[...]
His w[...]
workir[...]
Plains[...]
somet[...]
once [...]
seven[...]
perioc[...]
diova[...]
tivitie[...]
peare[...]

A[...]
anoth[...]
the o[...]
eight[...]
costs[...]
enon[...]

A[...]
his 4[...]

and Ruth's income, which was clearly insufficient. Despite this, Alva was fortunate. He had a wife, twenty years his junior, who was able to work and care for him. Had he not, he would have become a ward of the state and been confined to a convalescent hospital.

Insurance paid for all but 2,500 dollars of various surgeries. Ruth made regular, though small, payments over seven years to reduce their debt. The payments were made from her 150 dollars-a-week salary as a cook in a private club.

Alva's case somehow came to the attention of the U.S. Senate Special Committee on Aging. Ruth was asked to testify before the committee in 1987 as it considered Catastrophic Health Care Costs.

In her testimony, Ruth noted that during the years she kept Alva at home after his initial surgeries, she frequently arrived home from work to find he had fallen and had been lying on the floor for hours. On one occasion he had broken ribs; on another a broken leg.

"Then one day I came home and found him and he could not talk to me; he could not even drink water. He was completely paralyzed. He knew everything that was going on and at that time he could not speak. I called our family doctor and he came right over. That is when he told me 'Ruth, you cannot keep him at home any longer.'

"I told my doctor, 'I cannot tell him he is going to a nursing home; you will have to do it.' So he told Alva he would have to go to a convalescent home until he could take care of himself, which we knew he could never do.

"But he was willing to go, and I guess I am fortunate in this. I have a wonderful nursing home that he is in and he has never asked me to come home.

"Since he has been in the nursing home, he has had two or three more strokes. Once in a while he can talk to you, but mostly it is just a whisper.

"He says, 'I do not like you to be working as hard as you are.' And I tell him, 'You took care of me all these years. I will take care of you now.' But it is getting to the point where I do not know. Now his Social Security check is 498 dollars. I will have to be paying the nursing home a little more, because he got an increase. He only gets 25 of the 498 dollars.

"He does take five . . . drugs, but only two that have to be written by the doctor. The others . . . you can buy over the counter. I have to pay for that, and I have to pay for his personal belongings and to have his hair cut and things like that, which is more than the 25 dollars."

Ruth is supposed to take high blood pressure medicine and a heart pill four times a day, but she has not been able to afford them. She has a damaged cartilage in her knee that needs to be repaired, and which is especially problematic because she is on her feet all day cooking. Her eyeglasses have not been changed in seven years. Ruth, at age sixty-eight, does not see her golden years as very appealing.

Ruth and Alva's life savings were exhausted in the first six months of his stay in the convalescent home. At the time of her testimony, her bill at the druggist was 1,300 dollars. She owes their former doctor 1,500 dollars. Fortunately, he is not pressing them for it. She has let her car and home insurance lapse. For eighteen years, Ruth maintained a hospitalization supplement policy, but had to drop it in order to cope with past due bills.

The case of Alva and Ruth is not unusual. We are aware of many such situations and House and Senate files are filled with similar cases. The question is "What do we do when we go to the well and the well is dry?"

The hard questions are "How serious is the situation? What is being done about it? And finally, what else can be done?"

HOW SERIOUS IS THE SITUATION?

The White House, in a statement entitled "The President's Initiative On Catastrophic Illness Coverage," issued in 1987, stated:

"The urgency of long-term care is an increasingly important issue. By the year 2030, an estimated 8.6 million Americans will be over age 85, compared to 2.7 million in 1985.

"About 1.4 million elderly now receive care in nursing homes, at an average expense of over $22,000 a year. [Most of] These costs are not covered by Medicare or private insurance, although many elderly and their families are under the impression they are. Of the $32 billion in 1985 nursing home costs, less than 2 percent was paid by private insurance. Of the remainder, half was paid out of savings by patients and their families and the other half was covered by Medicaid.

"Virtually all elder Americans are entitled to acute care coverage under Medicare. Nearly two-thirds also supplement their coverage with so-called 'Medigap' policies purchased in the private insurance market.

"Medicare is designed as an acute care coverage program. Much of the cost of physician services and hospital stays under 60 days are covered. Longer hospital stays are not fully covered and prescription drugs are not covered at all. Some Medigap policies cover those additional expenses, but many do not.

"The major source of fear for the elderly is that they could be faced with expenses that are not covered either by Medicare or Medigap. In addition, confusion often exists over what acute care coverage the elderly have and do not have. Some elderly buy too much insurance, while other believe they have more coverage than they actually have."

We believe it is unfortunate and shortsighted of our government not to take into account the lack of coverage for in-home care. Much of the $22,000 average annual cost of maintaining an individual in a nursing or convalescent care facility could be reduced through in-home care. In many cases these costs can be dramatically reduced.

We have seen a substantive increase in the use of in-home care in recent years. As we mentioned earlier, this is caused in large measure by the enactment of the Omnibus Reconciliation Act of 1980, which removed certain acute care reimbursement provisions and sent people home from the hospital quicker . . . and often sicker.

This legislation also removed the limit on the number of covered home health visits, eliminated the requirements for prior hospital stays, and allowed more home health agencies to participate in the program.

Thus, home health expenditures between 1980 and 1984 went from $800 million to $1.6 billion. In

1985, that figure rose to $2.4 billion and, according to figures provided by the Health Care Finance Organization, are expected to rise to $4 billion in 1990. Similarly, the number of home health visits increased by 78 percent from 1980 to 1985.

The number of agencies participating in the providing of in-home health care has jumped from 2,900 in 1980 to 6,000 in 1986.

SOMETHING IS HAPPENING

Yet, it is important to point out that the Medicare home health benefit is not a long-term care benefit for chronically ill individuals. It does not pay for all services provided by homemakers or nurses aides. That means huge numbers of people are still left out of the coverage loop.

Further, the presidential comments, while laudable in the general sense, do not appear to take into consideration the fact that millions of Americans between the ages of sixty-five and eighty-five (with eighty-five cited in the statement) also require long-term health care. What about these people?

And nothing is said about the many individuals who are stricken prematurely by strokes, head injuries from auto accidents, ALS (Lou Gehrig's disease), multiple sclerosis, AIDS, and countless other situations that require costly long-term care.

Is the situation critical? Consider the statements of others from various Congressional hearings.

"When I visit senior centers or hold town meetings in my state, the one issue that comes up time and time again is the cost of health care," says U.S.

Senator Bill Bradley (D.—N.J.).

"During our hearings . . . I was truly amazed by some of the testimony presented by our witnesses. These witnesses are hard working, honest, middle-class Americans who had become impoverished by a catastrophic illness. These individuals had taken out Medicare supplement policies and even saved a portion of their earnings for such an emergency. Despite these preparations, they found themselves totally broke and heavily in debt from medical expenses arising from catastrophic illness. Many had to put off their own needed medical care so they could have money for their loved ones. These witnesses represent mainstream America and illustrate the severity of the problem," according to U.S. Senator Larry Pressler (R.—S.D.).

"The lack of a comprehensive long-term care system which encompasses medical, social, and personal care services provided in a variety of community, home-based and institutional settings is the greatest deficiency in our present health care delivery system. There is greater pressure than ever to search out private financing mechanisms to meet the very substantial and rapidly escalating costs associated with the delivery of long-term care services," notes the American Association of Retired Persons.

And the Health Insurance Association of America suggests that "Financial protection against the costs of long-term care may well become the dominant financing issue in the coming decades."

The die is cast. There is agreement between the public and private sectors that the need for a comprehensive program to provide for the health-care needs of Americans of all ages and walks of life is more than evident; it is crying out for action.

FEDERAL LEGISLATION

While progress is frustratingly slow, there is progress. Senate and House Committees have been holding hearings for at least four years. In doing so, these members of the Congress have been educating themselves to the many problems our citizens are confronting and, in the process, the eyes of many of these legislators have been opened. Most are of an age where they will personally be confronted with some of these problems in the near term. Many have been able to identify with the situations presented to them because they have loved ones who are suffering. The testimony has brought things very close to home.

While there are good steps in the right direction, our major concern is that many, many agencies do not fall under the Medicare or Medicaid programs. Many people will continue to be shortchanged and/or victimized.

The greatest drawback in recent legislation proposed by the president, and the Catastrophic Health Care Bill passed and then repealed by the House and Senate, is they do not contain provisions to deal with long-term nursing home and in-home health care.

We can expect to see continued revisions in existing health-care legislation over the next several years.

This will take place if for no other reason than the fact that as our nation's population ages and grows in size, that segment of the population will continue to make themselves heard and will demand action from our legislators. The American Association of Retired Persons (AARP) purports to represent some 25 million Americans over age fifty. Hardly an issue of the AARP News Bulletin goes by without a major story on page one related to health-care legislation. Their lobbying efforts on Capital Hill are substantive and the organization is regarded as reputable and reliable; they are listened to.

THE INSURANCE INDUSTRY

What we used to refer to as the insurance industry is attempting to change its image. Many segments now refer to themselves as the financial services industry and agents now offer a variety of programs including mutual funds, stocks, government bonds, and certificates of deposit (CDs) as part of their portfolio of products. The standard insurance designation of CLU (Chartered Life Underwriter) is being replaced or added to with CFP (Certified Financial Planner) or CFP (Chartered Financial Planner).

Some interesting things are happening in health-care coverage as a result.

Some companies are now beginning to offer younger people a program that combines several traditionally separate forms of investment which will provide for catastrophic illness care the same way they now provide disability coverage, especially for self-employed people.

Others are beginning to experiment with long-term care coverages for people over age sixty-five. Because these policies have little or no history, they are constantly being revised. One insurance man referred to them as "second-generation products."

Our sources came up with no less than one hundred companies providing some form of long-term care coverage. Some companies are well known, some are not. Policies differ substantially and exclusions are often complex. Most of these policies, at present, are expensive and, in our judgment, wholly inadequate. Furthermore, to determine what is covered and what isn't requires a greater level of understanding of insurance than most Americans possess. Although progress may be slow, increasing attention is being given to the need. Of the companies we surveyed;

- Most provide from ten to fifty dollars a day in nursing-home benefits and the length of coverage may be up to four years. However, these policies included numerous pre-conditions and criteria before coverage could be implemented.
- Most provide no coverage or very little coverage for in-home health care.
- Most do not provide custodial care coverage.
- Most require prior hospital stay, thus eliminating a great many people.

Insurance firms, and the associations to which most belong, are continuing to work with the AARP and a variety of public sector organizations, including colleges and universities, to develop studies that would help provide answers to some of the problems facing their industry.

The need is great. Before we have obtained the answers and enacted and funded the legislation, a large number of individuals will continue to suffer financially because of the huge financial burden long-term health care imposes. Some will die needlessly and many will live the last years of their lives in depressing and deplorable circumstances.

WHAT ELSE CAN BE DONE?

First, we believe the cause of long-term health care must become a primary national priority. This means including both nursing home and in-home care, with coverage of skilled care and custodial care whether infirmity was caused by accident, illness, or simply age.

Second, we must develop a partnership between the public and private sectors that will permit a much larger share of our populace to receive the care they deserve without having to bankrupt themselves financially.

Third, we believe government and the financial services industry, which includes health insurance, must intensify its efforts to come up with imaginative new and affordable programs to allow more people to participate in funding their own health care.

For instance, if we can fund an IRA (Individual Retirement Account) and have it tax deferred, should we not also be able to fund an IHIP (Individual Health Indemnity Program), which has tax incentives and allows individuals to set aside funds for long-term chronic illnesses. We believe tax incentives should be provided to encourage the development of residential care facilities as long as staff training requirements are developed.

And fourth, we must mobilize action by the people of the United States who are currently affected by the financial and emotional costs of health care and generate articles in publications and discussion on talk shows, such as, "20/20," and "60 Minutes." We must raise the consciousness of the public at large and make health care a visible issue. Health care concerns cut across all social, racial, economic, and religious lines.

Solving the problem of how health care will be paid for, and providing an assurance that everyone in need will be able to receive care when needed, while assuring quality of life in our golden years, will go a long way to alleviating many of the other problems related to health care detailed in this book.

ROSEMARIE AND JUAN

Even when one is deeply involved in the care of elderly people on a daily basis and aware of the problems that confront relatives of these people, one can find oneself in difficult situations. One of the authors of this book did, as evidenced in the following story.

Rosemarie and Juan, now in their eighties, have been health gurus since they were in their twenties. They shied away from preservatives and sugars and didn't eat meat. They have led a "back to nature" kind of meditative life for close to sixty years and didn't believe in doctors.

Rosemarie was the solid, driving force. She always handled the family finances, drove the car, and provided leadership in the relationship.

Recently, when Rosemarie had a stroke and collapsed on the floor, Juan took her to the hospital.

Despite the fact that Rosemarie and Juan lived a very simple life, had built their own house of adobe bricks, and grew most of their own food, Rosemarie had handled their funds very shrewdly and they were not wanting financially.

When Rosemarie was discharged from the hospital, she and Juan were provided two choices, a convalescent hospital or in-home care. They elected to go home. Juan, however, soon began to resent the fact that Rosemarie needed continual care and her situation disrupted what had been a very private lifestyle. He had a set pattern that had been disturbed by doctors, medications, a hospital bed in one room, and nurses present twenty-four hours a day.

He became critical of the nurses for wearing makeup and for other personal habits. He began to throw Rosemarie's medicines out as they were contrary to the beliefs he had lived by for many years.

At first, he reluctantly accepted the fact that Rosemarie had had a stroke, but as time went by, he came to the misguided conclusion that it had not been a stroke. Rosemarie simply had been eating the wrong foods and she didn't need the medicines doctors had prescribed for the heart and stroke conditions. He forced Rosemarie to fast, would not let the nurses feed her, and began to force the nurses out. Rosemarie therefore would find herself alone from twelve to fourteen hours at a time.

She quickly developed bedsores all along her

back because she was not being turned and her skin was not being treated.

Despite the fact that we operate a caregiving service and Juan and Rosemarie were close relatives, our counsel and our services were being rejected.

And despite the familial relationship, they were deeply distrustful of revealing anything about their finances. After some digging, we discovered where they had their banking connections. Juan not only didn't know how much money they had or where it was being kept, he didn't know how to handle and balance a checkbook.

Forgetful, resentful, and angry over the disruption in his life and having to handle his own finances, Juan began to berate the caregivers even more, now accusing them of taking things that he had misplaced. He would hide things in secret drawers in old chests and not remember where he put them. On one occasion he accused someone of taking his worn-out old gardening pants.

It took every ounce of our patience to continually inform Juan in detail of what options were available and what his finances were. We explained that we could handle all the things that were making him uncomfortable. Eventually we won Juan over, but it took a year of constant explanation to wear away distrust and confusion. Patience proved the key.

Rosemarie, too, fought the situation from the beginning. She initially rebelled against the nurses. However, with great resignation, she ultimately agreed to allow someone to care for her. But the tension that had developed between Rosemarie and Juan forced us to move Rosemarie to a good nursing home where she is being well cared for. We do provide weekly monitoring of her condition by regular visits of our public health nurse. Juan's stresses have been reduced and he remains at home.

9. A Call to Action

The picture we have painted in the first eight chapters of *Hidden Shame* is not positive.

We have provided you with many case histories of real people who have suffered, often needlessly. They represent hundreds of thousands of others whose stories couldn't be told here. But we all know people like these; they are our fathers and mothers, our aunts, uncles, and friends. They are our husbands and wives, brothers, and sisters. They are us.

We focused upon the reality of the fact that in the years ahead, the number of people who will be over sixty-five in the U.S. will represent the largest segment of our population and they will be living longer. Their health-care needs will also tax our ability to provide for them and pay for the services rendered.

We have brought to your attention the often well-meaning, but frequently inadequate and detrimental actions of attorneys, accountants, bank trusts officers, and friends; actions that we believe, in many cases, have shortened life or significantly reduced the quality of life of an individual.

We pointed out the frightening prospect of hiring a parasite rather than a trained, concerned, and caring health aide.

We highlighted the need to have uniform training and certification of home health aides and aides in nursing and residential care homes.

We discussed the inadequacies of the Medicare and Medicaid systems as related to nursing home and in-home health care and noted how quickly an individual's life savings can be lost once they develop a chronic long-term illness.

We showed you how elderly people unable to fend for themselves can lose their rights to make their own decisions and have those decisions made by a stranger.

We detailed abuse and neglect, intentional and unintentional, by family members as well as others; abuse that may be physical, emotional, psychological, or financial.

We highlighted the efforts of Congress and citizen's action groups to draw to the attention of our nation's leaders the plight of the elderly ill—and of how little has been done to actually alleviate the problem.

The picture is a real one. It is, in fact, worse than what we have portrayed.

The picture was drawn for a purpose. We believe it often takes hard, straight talk to jar the American people out of complacency, into an understanding of what is happening around them and, more particularly, what can and *will* happen to them or someone near them, if nothing is done.

Our message has been repeated in one form or another in each chapter. This one is no exception. That message is to plan ahead. Obtain information about the circumstances surrounding your health and that of your loved ones *before* a crisis arises. Develop a plan to deal with such situations based on the facts, on knowledge, and on reality.

Having said all that, are we naysayers, full of

doom and gloom? Decidedly not. To the contrary. We believe in living life to its fullest, in developing our individual potential, and in helping people to enjoy a better quality of life through the administration of quality health care. We have dedicated our personal and professional lives to that cause.

Because of that, we tend to see the positive side of things in most of life. But when we see things that are out of whack, which create situations that we cannot put up with, when we see injustice and indecision, lack of human caring, and the presence of human suffering where suffering need not exist, we can become advocates for a better route through the health-care maze.

In this, the final chapter of *Hidden Shame*, we are issuing a call to action.

We believe too many people are affected by a lack of adequate health-care funding, too many people will be affected in the future and the residual effects in terms of lost resources, and emotional and financial damage to families will be enormously draining if nothing is done.

If we have been concerned about what has happened to our family farmers and what is happening to our educational system, then we need to pay special attention to the problem of health care because it will affect far greater numbers of us in myriad ways.

And when you get right down to it, shouldn't health care be a fundamental human right for all Americans? Can we justify turning away people in need based on pure economics?

As we pointed out in Chapter 2, we are in the middle of a health-care revolution. And, as Winston Churchill allegedly pointed out regarding the conduct of World War II, "the war is too important to be left to the generals." We suggest the war against inadequate health care for Americans is also too important to leave to the American Medical Association and the insurance industry.

We need to involve ourselves in the fray. We need to stand up and have our collective voices heard. We need to be in touch with our congresspersons and our state legislators. They *do* listen.

We need to educate ourselves and to learn to sort out the facts. The scenarios often are confusing and the number of organizations with axes to grind are legion.

How can we do that? First, try contacting the House and Senate Committees on Aging. Find out what legislation is being considered on long-term health care. Ask for copies of the bill or of a summary of the bill so you will know what is being considered. Review the proposed legislation and then express your support or concern to the various legislators who are on the committees and copy your letters to your own congressman and senator. And write often.

If you have a case story that dramatizes the point you wish to make, volunteer to appear before House or Senate hearings, in Washington or locally, to share your story.

When you have arrived at an understanding of the legislation and have established a position, talk to others you know who might be affected by the legislation. Urge them to mobilize their energies in support of or in opposition to the legislation.

Then write—and urge others to write—to the president urging him to support your position. In Washington, it is generally true that the squeaky wheel gets the grease. Make yourself heard!

Become part of a larger movement. You might find the American Association of Retired Persons (AARP) an organization you could support. They have an active and well-funded lobbying program and have a staff of people who are well versed on health-care subjects. Ask to be placed on their mailing list.

Then, as you learn about their positions on various issues, let them know how you feel about those positions.

There are numerous other organizations whose efforts need your support.

The National League For Nursing is advancing nursing education and nursing practice to provide quality and affordable health care to consumers. It operates throughout the nation and works to develop effective and efficient health policy by providing information to legislators and administration officials on a variety of health-care programs.

Since the bulk of long-term health care is provided by or under the supervision of registered nurses and licensed vocational (or practical) nurses, support of the activities of the NLN is vital to our future health-care delivery system.

The NLN, with headquarters in New York City, has an extensive list of publications that provide valuable information for anyone interested in health care, particularly in community health and home care.

Another organization providing valuable information and counsel in the health-care field is the American Association of Homes for the Aging, in Washington, D.C.

This organization provides important guidelines

on continuing care retirement communities, publishing thoughtful papers on such subjects as the aging of America, Medicare and Medicaid at the crossroads, and shaping the future of America's elderly.

In your town or neighborhood there may be organizations such as the Alliance on Aging that can provide you with information that will help you to make informed decisions on health care policy. Attend debates and discussions. Get people talking about health care.

The point we are trying to make here is that there is an ever-growing awareness of the plight of America's elderly ill and that there are organizations of all types all across the nation which are banding together to demand action on critical issues. There is strength in numbers and you and we need to be part of those numbers.

The role of the elderly in our society and the inseparable twin subjects of gerontology and health care have been the subject of many nationally distributed articles in such publications as the *Wall Street Journal* and *Time*. The national wire services have dealt with various aspects of the subject. In late 1987, a major health-care legislative proposal related to catastrophic illness was considered by Congress, championed in part by the Administration.

But now is not the time to be satisfied. Attention to this problem quickly can be redistributed to other causes. It is too easy to think that all this exposure will suffice to make things happen and we need no longer mobilize forces to take action.

Nothing could be further from the truth.

The enormity of the problem needs to be brought home again and again. Creative solutions to health-care needs require the attention of our best minds. The challenge to our federal and state budgets will not only tax our existing resources, but those of generations to come.

We must not only find ways of providing quality health care to all who need it—in acute care centers, in nursing home and residential care facilities, and at home—but we must examine how our health-care dollars are spent in other areas and make some tough decisions.

What kind of questions are forcing these tough decisions?

Former Colorado Governor Richard Lamm posed such questions in his article in the May/June 1987 issue of *The Humanist.* In asking "How can we make our health care delivery system more efficient?" and "How do we use the capital we have to build a better life for our children?" Lamm offers several "commandments" of health care that are admittedly controversial. We do not agree with everything he says, but he does make suggestions that stimulate discussion. Our hope in presenting some of them here is to get you thinking.

Lamm notes that we are currently spending more for health care than we are for education and that health-care expenditures are growing at a faster rate than defense expenditures.

"We are great at treating sick people, but poor at treating a sick economy.

"Like the person who carries a first-aid kit, the weight of which gives him blisters, our health-care system has become part problem, part solution. We wouldn't want to be without it, but is has become a heavy burden. Health-care insurance now costs U.S.

corporations approximately 50 percent of their profits before taxes. That's money that is desperately needed elsewhere."

Controversial thinking? You bet!

Part of what Lamm is leading up to is a reordering of our decision-making process. Decisions such as whether we should continue to concentrate on extending lives of people when they cannot lead lives of reasonable quality. An example would be the forty-year-old person in a coma, brain dead.

Lamm and William L. Kissick, Professor of Public Health and Preventive Medicine at the University of Pennsylvania, suggest that we are too conditioned to think of health care in terms of doctors and hospitals and we must adjust our thinking.

Lamm and authors William Schwartz and Rudolf Klein (*The Painful Prescription*) warn us that health care as we know it now will continue to be rationed. Some people will receive it; some won't in the future. Lamm suggests that instead of lamenting the fact, we should ask ourselves how we might allocate finite resources to meet an infinite demand and do it with compassion and in fairness. Another tough question.

In another example, Lamm points out that Humana Hospital's budget for their artificial-heart program is roughly equivalent to what the U.S. spent on eradicating smallpox. He notes that we have a tendency as a society to direct funds to highly dramatic technology rather than to where the dollars might do the most good for the most people.

It is not our purpose to debate with Governor Lamm. But we are concerned with the people we see and come into contact with and whom we can project will be in need of health-care services in the future.

144

We are concerned about the people—and hundreds of thousands of others like them—whose cases are represented in this book. They are America's hidden shame, our elderly ill, who are not protected by Medicare or Medicaid or any other aid.

Professor Kissick, talking about health care in the '80s, noted that de Tocqueville observed in his book *Democracy in America*, published in the 1800s, that America has a plethora of special interest groups. He was right then and today those special interest groups have grown in numbers and in influence.

In health care, the alphabet organizations such as the American Medical Association (AMA), etc., are being joined by countless and often well-funded consumer interest groups. He cites such diverse organizations as the American Legion and the Gray Panthers, HealthPac, the Committee for National Health Insurance, and the Washington Bureau Group on Health.

These are organizations that understand and practice citizen advocacy. They all have a point of view and each of us will have to pick and choose which organizations best speak to our interests as they relate to health care in the future.

Every great social change in our history has come as a result of citizen involvement at the grass roots level: the American Revolution; the abolition of slavery; child labor laws; the right of women to vote; the civil rights movement . . . all evolved because enough people believed in and advocated an idea whose time had come.

We believe the time has come for a major revision in the way our nation looks at health care, how it is

145

delivered, and how it is paid for. We believe it must start with care provided to the elderly and that one way to correct some of the current imbalances is to permit people to receive in-home care in a more humane, efficient, and less costly manner.

And if we are to accomplish that step, it will require a virtual army of individuals who, recognizing the need and the burden the unfulfilled need presents to us, are willing to mobilize and create the change required. We have hope. After all, as the great Greek Heraclitus noted so long ago, "Nothing is permanent except change."